HOLE IN MY FAMILY PORTRAIT

ENDORSEMENTS

This book offers an honest and unfiltered glimpse into a mother's grieving process. Women who have experienced the loss of a child will find it helpful and replayable. I'm proud of Jane for opening up her heart with such honesty and vulnerability.

—Jim Daly, President, *Focus on the Family*

Having lost my only child to murder, I can tell you this inspirational story will remind you that God holds the world in the palm of his hand, and it's possible to go from grief to grace after child loss. This mother's bond with God is an excellent example of how God's grace will help anyone suffering from loss.

If you place your anxiety into the arms of Jesus, the peace of God will wash over you. *Hole in My Family Portrait* will show you how to put your hope in God when you face life's storms and praise God even when the unimaginable happens—like losing a child.

—Tammy Horvath, author of *Gone in an Instant: Losing My Son, Loving His Killer*

Regardless of the losses you have experienced, you will be touched by this book in powerful ways. Instead of hopelessness from your loss, you will know God cares about you. Instead of believing lies about "the perfect way to grieve," you will give yourself permission to grieve in your own way. Instead of misinterpreting the awkward ways people try to help you, you will be gracious toward those who hurt you. Though you may shed some tears like I did as you read this book, your heart will feel hopeful and comforted knowing God's presence. No matter where you are in your grief journey through the dark tunnel of loss and loneliness, Jane Daly's *Hole in My Family Portrait* will bless you. Her book is filled with honesty, vulnerability, and compassion for her readers. I highly recommend it. Read it for yourself and read it to be able to minister to others.

—Kathy Collard Miller, international speaker and bestselling award-winning author of over sixty books, including *Pure Hearted: The Blessings of Living Out God's Glory* (www.KathyCollardMiller.com)

With raw and heartfelt honesty, Jane Daly opens the door to the intimate intersection of diagnosis, grief, and God. In the isolating depths of grief, this book becomes a lifeline for mothers who've lost children, reminding them they're not alone—even in the face of the worst news, hope endures.

Daly fearlessly tackles the hard questions, providing rare insights into unspoken thoughts and feelings about God, distinguishing this book. It's a relatable narrative, regardless of whether we've walked the exact path as the author.

From the delicate balance of loss and faith, Jane writes, offering the stark choice: turn away from God or draw near and trust. I'm grateful she chose the latter. In her wholly honest story, Jane extends hope, comfort, and a haven for women who share the painful journey of losing a child.

—Karen Brough, author of *I Can't Believe They're Gone: a kid's grief book that hugs, helps, and gives hope*

This heartbreaking journey of a mother whose son endured cancer as a youth, then faced a losing battle with it in his thirties, gave me insight to the unrelenting grief one suffers from the death of a loved one. Jane Daly shares her agonizing saga, moving from grief to the point of realizing she could choose to be a victim of circumstances or a recipient of God's grace. Honest and conversational, this book can be a lifeline for anyone who wonders if the pain will ever go away. Personally, her insights helped me understand how long the devastation of grief may take to subside so I can better support a grieving friend.
—**Pamela Rosales**, coauthor of *Ghetto Boy, A Memoir*

Hole in My Family Portrait is a deeply personal account of one mother's grief following the sickness and death of her adult son. Her honesty and authenticity make this book a must-read for everyone, not just those who have experienced a similar loss, but for those who may not know how to comfort a friend who is experiencing loss.
—**Linda Wood Rondeau**, author of *Lessons Along the Way*

Jane S. Daly's memoir of a mother's love riven by grief is a stunning portrayal of God's unwavering grace unto healing—her son Bobby's ultimate healing and hers, still ongoing. Confident her loving Father allows her to grieve freely, Daly makes no apologies for her aching transparency or raw emotions. She doesn't try to compare her experience with that of others either, which adds to the story's poignant authenticity. Daly crafted this memoir years after her son died. By God's grace, those long years afforded her a broader perspective and deeper wisdom. I offer my highest endorsement for *Hole in My Family Portrait*.
—**Clarice G. James**, award-winning author of women's contemporary fiction

Jane Daly's experience bolsters us during the hardest days.
—**Nick Harrison**, author of *The One-Year Life Recovery Prayer Devotional*

With beautifully crafted words and an open heart, Daly takes us sailing on an unforgettable journey that ends where it began—in the loving arms of a God who was with her every step of the way.

—**Patrick E. Craig**, author of *The Apple Creek Dreams* series

Honest. Straightforward. Authentic. I was struck by Jane Daly's honesty about grieving. Whether a parent, spouse, or an adult child whose loved one died, Jane shares the journey we all have been on. She openly tells us her thoughts about religious platitudes and what seems like a lack of understanding of the painful time. In the end, Jane reveals how she healed, which helps us the reader know how we can travel through the darkness of grief to the light of Jesus.

—**Susan K. Stewart**, author of *Donkey Devos: Listen When God Speaks* www.susankstewart.com

HOLE IN MY FAMILY PORTRAIT

JANE DALY

ELK LAKE PUBLISHING INC®

PUBLISHING THE POSITIVE
Plymouth, Massachusetts

A Christian Company
ElkLakePublishingInc.com

COPYRIGHT NOTICE

Library Cataloging Data

Names: Daly, Jane (Jane Daly)

Hole in My Family Portrait / Jane Daly

148 p. 23cm × 15cm (9in × 6 in.)

ISBN-13: 9781649499929 (paperback) | 9781649499936 (trade paperback) | 9781649499943 (e-book)

Key Words: Grief and bereavement; death of a child; cancer; Christian living; family saga; grief recovery; loss of an adult child

Library of Congress Control Number: 2024932490 Nonfiction

DEDICATION

To Mike—You held my hand and pulled me along this journey. Thanks for your encouragement and love.

Table of Contents

ACKNOWLEDGMENTS

I am grateful for my husband, who encouraged me to tell this story. Although we both grieved in different ways, and still do, we acknowledge God is the One who numbers our days. We won't know this side of heaven why Bobby only lived thirty years, while my mom lived until the age of ninety-four.

I could not have written this book without the knowledge I will one day see Bobby again because of our mutual acceptance of Jesus Christ and his promise of eternal life.

A special thank you to Nick Harrison who asked me the question, "Have you ever thought about writing a book about your son's death?" We were the only two people sitting at the final dinner at the Oregon Christian Writers Summer conference (now Cascade Christian Writers). He encouraged me to get the story down to be a help to other mothers who have lost a child.

Finally, to every mother who has experienced the loss of a child—I see you. Your pain is real, and your struggle hasn't gone unnoticed. You are the strong ones, the ones who continue to live life despite your devastating loss. Please feel free to reach out to me for prayer or encouragement.

PREFACE

The death of a child has been called the greatest loss.

Nothing can prepare a mother for the passing of a child. A mother carries a baby inside for nine months. He's part of her. He shares her food and air. He feels his mother's emotions, hears her voice. They're connected by something greater than the slim tether of an umbilical cord.

Love at first sight becomes more than a romantic ideal. From the moment a baby is born, he's the sole object of her adoration. He's perfect, beautiful. He'll be the smartest, cutest, best baby ever born.

In this one brief moment, we mirror God, having created a person solely dependent upon us for everything. We get a glimpse—a better understanding—of God's great and sacrificial love for us as we sacrifice for our child. We have a firmer grasp of God's providential care as we provide for our child's needs.

As a baby grows, a mother is his world. When he cries, he wants his mother. When he's hungry, he needs his mother. When he falls and scrapes his knee, what's the first thing he says?

"I want my mommy!"

We foresee a bright, shiny future for our children. We want for them everything denied to us in the past. The opportunities we've let slip by, we grasp onto for our child.

Everything changes when they are snatched away.

Like a head-on collision, the world stops in an instant. We're initiated into a club whose membership we never asked for. A hole is created in us which can't be filled.

"You have other children," we're told.

As if he can be replaced—like telling an amputee, "You have another leg. What's the problem?"

We start the process of grief, and we either work through it, or it works on us. Trying to hold grief at bay is like trying to stand firm on a beach during a tsunami. When the tsunami warning sounds, we must seek the highest ground and climb to the top of the mountain.

Working through the process of grief is like the climb from the valley floor to the high point of hope through Christ. "Yea, though I walk through the valley of the shadow of death ..." (Psalm 23:4).

Death is only a shadow to the believer and our life a vapor. Mothers, if your child made a decision to follow Christ, take courage. You will see your beloved child again. God gave his Son so you could be with your son or daughter for all eternity.

Grief has been described as the feeling of being doused with kerosene and set on fire. Grief is having your heart removed while it's still beating. Grief is a sucker punch to the gut, a baseball bat to the head, a rug jerked out from beneath you. You lie comatose on the floor, wondering if you'll ever be able to breathe again—wondering if you even want to, and why.

In the darkest hour, in the deepest valley, when your life feels like it's leaking away because of sorrow, God is there. His grace brought you to this point, and his grace will sustain you. He'll dampen the flames, bandage the hurt, and put your heart back where it belongs.

But you'll be changed forever.

Breathe in his grace and let him wrap you in it. Like a warm, soft blanket on a rainy day, he will surround you and lift you back onto your feet.

I know. I've been there.

Come with me on this journey. Take my hand, and we'll journey together—from grief to grace.

CHAPTER 1

THE GOLDEN CHILD

"Your son's cancer is in remission."

I collapsed against the sofa, holding the phone in my sweaty hand. We'd been waiting for those words for nine long months. I hung up the phone and immediately called my husband, Mike, to tell him the news. He told me later that after my call, he went into a closet at work and wept.

Our son, Bobby, was diagnosed with Hodgkin's disease in September of the year he turned seventeen. He was the younger of our two children. He and his older sister, Heather, were born twenty months apart. Not our idea to have a second child so soon, but God had his plan.

Mike and I met at church in February of 1977. We went out five nights in a row, and then I left for a month-long tour of Europe with my parents and my grandmother. On my return, I was certain Mike had forgotten about me since he was the church's social butterfly. But God was working in both our hearts during our month apart. We fell in love with each other long-distance, with no contact at all. (Remember, cell phones and the internet didn't exist back then.)

After my return home on the first of April, we became engaged on the thirteenth. We married August 26, 1977.

Heather was born ten months later. A week after she was born, we moved to Sacramento so Mike could attend Bible school. We decided to hold off having another child until he graduated.

But as I said before, God had other plans. Somehow we managed to survive with two small children and one income—Mike's GI Bill and part-time job as a youth pastor. We had lots of help from my parents and grandmother, who moved to Sacramento too.

Before Bobby's diagnosis, we called him the Golden Child. He was gifted in many ways, and things came easily to him. He got good grades in spite of barely cracking open his books. He played football, basketball, and baseball for his Christian high school. His quick wit made him popular. He was homecoming prince his sophomore year. He seemed to have it all. When one of his many girlfriends did something for him or gave him an unexpected gift, we teased him mercilessly. "Golden Child syndrome," Heather would tell him. Bobby would shrug in a wordless gesture of *What can I say?*

Despite the title, her brother had been a handful. His strong will often clashed with us, his teachers, and school administrators. He looked at his world in strict black and white. Many times, he fought for the underdog, earning him respect from his classmates, but also earning the label of "rebellious" from the leadership of his Christian school.

At home, when his behavior required disciplining, he'd charm me out of being too strict. God doesn't place children in families by accident, but on more than one occasion I'd stated, "If Bobby had been born first, he'd be an only child."

By God's grace, he was born second.

During the summer leading up to his junior year of high school, he complained of pain in his back. We attributed it to a muscle sprain which probably happened while he was wakeboarding. Or mountain biking. Or during football practice.

Prior to the beginning of school, all football players were required to have a physical, so we scheduled the appointment with our family physician. A week or so before the appointment, Bobby asked me to feel some bumps in his neck. They felt like swollen glands. I told him he was probably fighting a cold, and to have the doctor feel them the following week.

The next week during football practice, Bobby broke a finger. How convenient as he was scheduled to see the doctor the next day. My husband took him to the appointment.

I was at work when Mike called.

"I don't want to alarm you, but the doctor took a needle biopsy of those lumps in Bobby's neck. He also found some swelling in the lymph nodes under his arm. I don't want you to worry."

I'm a mom. Worry is my middle name. Fear jolted through me, zapping me of the ability to pray. Bobby was my baby, my Golden Child.

That night, my husband and I attended our home Bible study, and I shared my concerns with the group. They assured me the lumps were probably nothing more serious than mononucleosis. They prayed over me, pleading the blood of Jesus, claiming healing in his name.

The doctor's office called my husband on Thursday, asking if we could meet with the doctor on Friday afternoon. The nurse wouldn't give Mike any information on the phone but just repeated the doctor needed to talk to all three of us.

Fear engulfed me.

The next afternoon we sat in the examination room, trying to assure each other everything would be fine. The three of us were adrift in a sea of anxiety as the doctor entered the room and closed the door. His face was grim.

"Your son has cancer."

Four words irrevocably changed my world.

My church taught parents had a moral duty to pray over their children, their homes, their finances, and their health. If you prayed fervently enough, bad things couldn't happen. You had to have faith. Spiritual warfare wasn't taken lightly.

Apparently, I'd failed my son. Somewhere, my guard had gone down, and the enemy got past my defenses. My boy's cancer must have been my fault.

Depression sucked me into a bog of quicksand. The emotional pain turned into physical pain. All my joints swelled. Getting out of bed in the morning and getting dressed became an ordeal. I was convinced my ailments were God's punishment for my lack of diligence.

I asked God to let me die. I felt as if he'd forgotten about me. If I was his child, how could this happen?

When I was first saved at the age of twenty-one, my naïve thought was my life would be even better than it had been. Mike often teased me about my Pollyanna upbringing. My grandparents always lived close by and were my regular babysitters. Both my parents and grandparents were married to the same person for their entire adult lives. My father never had a period of unemployment. Although we weren't wealthy, I had everything I needed, and many things I wanted. We took trips to Disneyland. My grandmother often took me to plays and concerts to expand my cultural experiences. She taught me to sew and to cook. When I learned how to drive, she gladly handed me her keys whenever we'd go somewhere.

There were few bumps in my life's road.

Though I'd never had to win my father's approval, somewhere along the way, God's approval had seemingly become based upon my conduct. If I adhered to the dos and don'ts of Scripture, God would rain blessings upon me. We disconnected our television, listened only to Christian music, and didn't go to any movie rated higher than PG. We faithfully tithed 10 percent of our meager income, attended church every Sunday morning, Sunday night, and Wednesday night. I sang in the choir. We led a youth group. I got up at five thirty every morning to read my Bible and pray before the kids awoke.

All these works for God's blessings, yet my teenage son got cancer. How could this be?

Overwhelmed by our own pain, watching our son getting sicker from chemo, my husband and I stopped attending church. We felt shunned by those believers whose faith was stronger. We were outcasts. Despite our prayers, tithes, worship, and service, our son was ill. We must have unconfessed sin in our lives. Our church body didn't know how to respond to our pain. No one called to see why we weren't in church—not even the pastor.

Where was God? How could he have allowed this thing to happen?

St. John of the Cross, in his famous poem, describes the "dark night of the soul." The main idea is about the difficulties we endure as we seek to grow in union with God. This dark night is described as a feeling God has left us. Prayer, which used to come easily, now feels forced and empty.

Such was my experience as I lay awake in the dark, mentally watching my words of entreaty bounce off the ceiling and fall back on me like dry leaves.

Bobby's prognosis was good. Even though his cancer was stage four Hodgkin's, it was curable—six days of chemo, followed by three weeks of recovery before another round—a total of three rounds of chemo. I drove him every day and sat in one of the comfy recliners, reading or watching TV, as chemicals were forced into my son's body through a Broviac port inserted in his chest. The first couple of days were the worst. He'd lie in the recliner, wrapped in a comforter to help with the chills racking his body. He'd have to get up, grab the rod holding the chemo bag, and dash for the bathroom to throw up.

Sometimes, Heather came and sat with us after her college classes, and Mike came as often as he could. He worked in a commission-only job at that time, so if he wasn't making a sale, he wasn't getting paid. Our family rallied around our shared outrage at the awfulness of our Golden Child's illness.

God was faithful to us by sending angels disguised as friends, bringing food during chemo. Other friends from Bobby's school organized a fundraising walk to help us with our financial needs. Our school community supported us, even though our church family abandoned us.

After the brutal course of three rounds of chemo and six weeks of radiation, the cancer was defeated. I had my son back.

Though hard to imagine anything good coming out of the situation, the best part for me was the time I got to spend alone with my son. Five days a week, for six weeks, we rode together to radiation. We'd laugh about a song which seemed to come on the radio at the same time every day.

Bobby was asked to speak to an elementary class in our neighborhood about his ordeal. He brought a message of hope and encouragement to the kids, even though he hated speaking in front of a group—something he inherited from his mother.

He loved sports, especially basketball. His skill on the court had won him a spot on the varsity team as a freshman. The juniors and seniors on the team liked and respected him, accepting his elevated status.

He hated not being able to play, but he inspired his fellow basketball players by showing up every afternoon to practice, even though he was exhausted from radiation. He suited up for every game and cheered his teammates on, though he didn't play at all that season.

Watching him, I began the slow crawl from the ocean of despair to the firm foundation of the shore.

***

American churches have unspoken expectations. We expect if we do certain things, God is obligated to bless. If we disobey, then God responds with a sharp rod. My view of God, formed by Bible-believing Christian saints, was of a God who dispensed blessings like a genie in a bottle. If I rubbed the bottle, said my prayers—in Jesus's name, of course—then I could expect God to pop out the desired blessing.

In Matthew 6:33, the Bible says, "But seek first the kingdom of God and His righteousness, and all these things shall be added to you." I looked for "all these things" to be added to me. The churches I attended as an adult didn't talk about God's blessings during trials. I was spiritually unprepared for the catastrophe of Bobby's cancer—running around a battlefield without any of the spiritual armor the Bible tells us is vital for our survival. I was naked and didn't even know.

After not attending church for a year, some dear friends asked us to come to their fellowship, a close-knit group of believers who lived out Philippians 2:13: "For it is God who works in you to will and to act in order to fulfill his good purpose" (NIV).

In the months following Bobby's remission, I discovered my life wasn't about performance. God wasn't my boss in the sky, evaluating my progress and grading me accordingly. I didn't have to do anything to be blessed by God. Bobby's cancer wasn't a punishment because I forgot to pray, didn't pray the right words, carried unforgiveness in my heart, or any other reason.

In John 9, the disciples asked Jesus why the man had been born blind. Who sinned, him or his parents? Jesus's response was, "Neither this man nor his parents sinned, but that the works of God should be revealed in him" (v.3).

I thought my faith was strong before Bobby's diagnosis. I'd prayed the prayer of faith many times and had seen God answer, sometimes miraculously. But when this tragedy struck, my faith withered quickly, like a plant without water.

My faltering steps toward understanding God's grace in every circumstance led me to strengthened faith. I would need that strength to meet the next challenge.

CHAPTER 2

THE CALL

When the phone rang that January evening in 2009, I had no idea my life was about to change forever. Mike picked up the phone and, as usual, put it on speaker. Bobby was calling.

"I need to talk to you and Mom."

I dried my hands while walking from the kitchen to the dining room, dread settling in my stomach like a stone. My instincts told me this wouldn't be a "Hey, I have great news!" kind of a call.

Bobby told us he'd been having health problems. Pressure in his chest. The doctors didn't know what was wrong, and a chest x-ray and MRI were inconclusive. He was going in for exploratory surgery in ten days.

He'd been well for eleven years. He was twenty-nine years old, healthy and active. His business was thriving, and he and his wife, Ali, had purchased their first home after five years of marriage. This would be a blip, something to fix and move on.

Surely his symptoms couldn't be cancer.

I flew to Colorado to be with him and Ali during the surgery. Bobby picked me up from the airport. On the way to his house, he asked, "Remember when I had cancer?"

I nodded.

"Remember how I broke my finger, and that's when they found the tumors?"

I nodded again, wondering where this was going.

His eyes met mine across the small interior of the car. "I broke my finger last week."

In that moment, I entered denial.

A group of us, including Ali's family and a few friends, gathered in the hospital waiting room. The doctor told us the surgery would be about four or five hours. We waited, watched the clock, updated those who couldn't be there, and worried. My prayers were selfish.

Please, God, let it be something fixable.

Eight hours later, we'd pestered the waiting room staff to the point of becoming belligerent. What was going on? Where was the doctor? Why couldn't someone tell us what was taking so long?

Finally, one of the surgeons entered the waiting room and made a beeline for our little group.

My hope was for some sign from the surgeon telling us all was well—a weary smile, a tired sigh—some kind of indication my baby was okay.

The doctor took a deep breath.

"Robert has a sarcoma growing in his chest cavity which is squeezing his lung. We tried to remove it, but it's spread out in such a way as to make it impossible."

Sarcoma?

The rest of his explanation evaporated into white noise. When he was finished, he asked if anyone had any questions. I raised my hand. Took a deep breath.

"Is it cancer?"

His answer was in the affirmative. Ali and I collapsed together and wept.

Alone in a private alcove, away from the crowd, I called Mike, barely able to squeeze out the words between gasps and sobs.

"Bobby has cancer."

Mike was on a plane to Colorado the next day.

Early on in our marriage, we'd decided divorce would never be an option for us. Whatever came at us, we'd face it, and with God's help, we'd find a way to make our marriage work. From time to time, issues arose from Mike's childhood with alcoholic parents and physical abuse. We'd been to counseling three times throughout the years.

When Bobby was first diagnosed with cancer at seventeen, we'd talked about how something like his illness might cause enough stress in a family to break it apart. We'd been—and still were—determined Satan wouldn't get a toehold in the situation.

Not even by putting us through it twice.

I also had a talk with Heather, since all the attention was focused on her brother. She was in her first year of college and in a serious relationship with a young man. She and Bobby had been best friends since they were little tykes, and she understood the gravity of her brother's illness. We often teased her because she called herself "The Good Child."

After the surgery, doctors discussed an aggressive chemo regimen, even though the prognosis was grim. Bobby's cancer was the rarest of rare, with a survival rate of 5 percent at five years. My thoughts ricocheted between hope and despair. I remember thinking, "I'm not going to be blindsided by this. I'll tell myself he's going to die, but hope he lives."

I kept a brave front. My tears were saved for the privacy of the guest room in Bobby's home.

He said something to me as startling as a splash of cold water. "I guess I'm going to have to live with this." Here I was, looking at death, while he was looking at life, even as he was gravely ill. He'd survived the last fight with the most dreadful of diseases.

Obviously, he'd decided he would survive again.

Heather flew out to spend a couple of days with us. We were allowed in Bobby's ICU room for ten minutes at a time.

"You could've found a better way to get everyone's attention," Heather told him. He smiled, unable to answer because of the pain.

They'd been as close as a brother and sister could be. When Mike and I were missionaries in rural Montana, some little boys Bobby's age lived across the street, and they'd knock on the door and ask if Bobby could come out and play. Many times Bobby would answer, "I just want to play with my sister." Those words became code between Mike and me when we didn't want to hang out with anyone else.

Bobby had come into the world after forty-five minutes of excruciating labor, all nine and a half pounds of him. He was a calm baby, sleeping through the night at only a few weeks. He took long naps and smiled all the time.

Something changed when he was two. The terrible twos lasted until he was an adult. He was strong-willed and stubborn, yet still sweet as only a little boy can be. As a child, he told me, "When I grow up, I'm going to live right next door to you, Mama."

Too bad a blonde-haired Colorado beauty caught his eye. Colorado was where he made his home and his life.

I was proud of the life he'd made for himself. He hated working for someone else, so starting his own business was a natural thing. His charm led him to win bids away from larger companies, and his strong work ethic earned him respect in his field.

During his recuperation from the sarcoma surgery, I called Bobby's best friend, Mark, and asked if he could come to Colorado to finish up some projects Bobby had going on. Mark was elated to be able to not only hang out with Bob-Dog, but to help in a tangible way. So, I went home, knowing Bobby and his business were in good hands, and made plans to return to Colorado when Bobby finished his first round of chemo.

God must have known I needed to spend as much time as possible with my son. His timing is always impeccable.

I'd been laid off from my job right before his surgery. The layoff was God's grace to me. My job was stressful, especially in light of the failing economy. Dealing with the pressure to perform at work, spend time with my son, and help take care of my aging parents would have been impossible.

The world kept spinning, day turning into night, but my corner of the world stopped. My focus during those first few days after Bobby's surgery became a familiar and comfortable routine. Get up, drive to the hospital, and sit in the waiting room until my turn came to spend five minutes with him in the intensive care unit. When he was released to a regular room, the routine changed very little, except then I sat in his room reading or talking quietly to family while he slept.

I'd like to say I spent hours in fellowship with God as Bobby recuperated, but the shock was too great. I pushed the pain away with a stiff arm in God's face. My mind needed to process the diagnosis. My bruised heart needed to be held and comforted.

But God was there, in spite of my rejection. Without his grace, I wouldn't have been able to function.

We humans are capable of amazing things in the face of tragedy. I was able to drop into autopilot and handle the mundane while reeling from the enormity of Bobby's situation. Meals had to be cooked for visitors. Laundry needed to be washed and cleaning to be done. Dogs needed to be walked.

I couldn't control the outcome of Bobby's life, but I could control necessary tasks, allowing Ali to tend to her husband.

How easily Mike and I slipped back into our role as parents. I grocery shopped and did errands, while Mike found things around the house needing repair. I cleaned and did housework, and he took care of routine car maintenance.

Life as usual, the comfort of having something to do, kept our minds off the devastating diagnosis. We stood at the edge of an emotional abyss, deep and dark and scary. We felt the hand at our back, pushing us forward, until we had no choice but to step off.

I did not then know how deep the valley of the shadow of death would be in the coming months.

CHAPTER 3

THE LONGEST YEAR

I didn't want to be known as the woman whose son died.

I pictured people whispering behind their hands—*that's her. She's the one.* A knowing nod, a sympathetic look. Pity. My mind clawed at the thought, desperate to escape a role I firmly rejected. I'm Bobby Daly's mom. The Golden Child's mother.

Not the mother of a dead boy.

"How's Bobby doing?" The question was asked hundreds of times by well-meaning people after my return from Colorado. My answer was always the same.

"Chemo's going okay. He's pretty sick. But we're hopeful."

There were no guarantees he'd be okay, but I still said it.

They looked relieved at my answer. They needed reassurance life is predictable. You get sick, doctors treat you, and you get well. You get cancer, you get chemo, and it works. Life goes on as usual.

I felt like a liar, playing into their need. Human beings, especially Christians, want assurance we're safe. The American Christian doctrine seems to be God loves you and has a wonderful plan for your life. Once you're born again, you're untouchable by all the tragedy in the world. In his book, *The Myth of the Modern Message,* Ray Comfort talks about how we entice unbelievers with a gospel implying Christianity will solve all their problems.

The reality is life isn't fair. Bad things happen to good people. Even twenty-nine-year-old men die of cancer. In car accidents. From guns. From carelessness. At their own hands.

Christians aren't immune to disaster.

As I write this, thousands of people, young and old, have become victims of accidental fentanyl overdoses. Some, like my friend Mary's son, needed relief from excruciating back pain. His cousin offered him a pill, neither of them knowing the words they exchanged then would be their last. Jacob was found unresponsive in his home by his wife. Imagine my friend's grief, knowing his death could have been prevented if his doctor could have provided something stronger than the prescription he was given.

I spoke with a young mother whose story cut deeply into my heart. She attended the same Christian school as Bobby and Heather. She and her husband looked forward with joy to the birth of their first child. Since they couldn't decide on his name, they called him Squirt.

Far along in her pregnancy came the news no woman wants to hear. Squirt wasn't developing the way he should. Weekly ultrasounds were ordered. At twenty-four weeks, the ultrasound revealed a chilling sight. The amniotic sac had ruptured, and the bands normally holding the sac in place had wrapped around Squirt and were squeezing him to death. The bands had already severed his fingers and were crushing his skull.

The images unfolding on the ultrasound screen were like scenes from a horror movie. Imagine knowing your baby would be born dead, killed by the very thing which was supposed to keep him safe.

She had to make the hardest decision of her life, to either let her child slowly and painfully die, or terminate the pregnancy—leaving the hospital with empty arms and an empty womb.

How did something like this happen to a young couple who loved God and were serving him through their church and their community? The greater question, though, is how can this mother still say she loves God and believes in his sovereign plan—even though the same thing happened to their unborn daughter a year later?

We want to make sense of stories like these. We struggle to find answers. We question why God allows such terrible things. We wonder at the seeming injustice of it all. We get what we don't think we deserve.

The World English Dictionary defines grace as the free and unmerited favor of God shown toward man. God's grace isn't all about the blessings of health, wealth, and prosperity, but rather about owning everything which comes our way—a paradigm shift.

Our American culture has changed the definition of grace to mean something God never intended. We struggle to believe good can come from bad circumstances. The salvation message is watered down, rendering it ineffectual to help us deal with suffering and loss.

How can the death of a loved one be "unmerited favor?"

I returned to Romans 8:28 time and time again during the year after Bobby's second diagnosis. "And we know that in all things God works for the good of those who love him, who have been called according to his purpose" (NIV). The answers to my questions were out there, but my view through the window was obscured by the dirt and grime of the sin and difficulty of the world. God's hope was on the other side of the window. I just couldn't see it yet. I had to cling to my faith, girded by his grace.

After Bobby was diagnosed, my prayers were a plea for God to help me deal with the outcome of Bobby's life—to help me find answers to my questions about life and unfairness, and if Bobby was to die, to assure me God would keep me in his hands. If Bobby was to be healed, I'd rejoice for the time we had left.

★★★

Facing devastating loss causes a shift in priorities. Things we once desired become of little value. We turn to introspection and reevaluation of what's important.

When I travel, I want to get from point A to point B in the shortest length of time. My goal is to get around all the slower moving traffic so as to get home quickly. One day, on the way home from the grocery store on a busy thoroughfare, a sad song came on the radio—"Fire and Rain" by James Taylor. I started to cry. Cars rushed around me because I'd slowed down and couldn't see through the tears. I wanted to yell out the window, "Can't you see my son is fighting for his life?" The urgency to get home wasn't important, not in light of the gravity of real life.

Our children go through hardships, and we watch as they grow and learn through their experiences. But this is something no parent wants to watch. How do you hold the tears in when your son loses twenty-five pounds during one round of chemo? Death was hovering, waiting, and I wanted to scream at it to go away. If there had been a way to change places with him, I would have done it in the space of a heartbeat.

I sat with Bobby a week after his first round of chemo. He'd just begun to feel better after the assault of poison to his bloodstream. He told me he was going to beat the disease, and I believed him.

We spent several days together, doing errands, hanging out, watching movies. His strength returned quickly. It was hard to believe he was ill. Friends and family stopped by to visit, and he received everyone with his typical cheerfulness, even though he didn't feel much like talking about what he was going through.

After the second round of chemo, his strength returned just as quickly. He invited a good friend and his two brothers-in-law over to help him shave his head. As the official photographer, I took pictures and laughed with them as they all shaved their heads in a gesture of solidarity. My tears would have to wait until later, captured inside until I was alone. My heart was full over the love shown among these young men.

We'd been waiting with combined dread and anticipation for the results of the CT scan. After two rounds of chemo, the doctor wanted to see if the tumor had responded. It had! We were euphoric. My emotional roller coaster of hope and despair—up, down, up—was on the upswing. The ride was beginning to make me sick. Getting off and returning to normal was my goal, my dream, my prayer.

I'd heard the phrase, "Everything happens for a reason." What could be the reason for cancer in a young person? Bobby was a good man, generous and loving. He made a profession of Christ as a boy and was baptized at eight years of age. What was the reason for a good man to die, while horrible people continue to commit crimes against children and still live? I remember reading in Matthew 5:45, "He causes his sun to rise on the evil and the good, and sends rain on the righteous and the unrighteous" (NIV).

There was a woman whose twelve-year-old daughter had drowned in their backyard swimming pool. They'd had no warning, no indication their beloved daughter would be snatched from them in an instant. She shared her story of arriving home to see police cars in front of their house. Their older daughter ran outside, screaming. She and her husband didn't know what to expect as they raced around the house to the backyard. A neighbor administered CPR, while police officers tried to hold them back. Too late. Andrea was gone.

In our conversation, she comforted me with her faith that God always knows what he's doing. Andrea's death didn't take God by surprise. Bobby's illness didn't accidentally slip God's attention either.

After hearing her story, I was glad to have the time to prepare for the worst outcome.

I had become a follower of Jesus Christ at twenty-one—old enough to have lived a life not pleasing to God. I'd been a sinner. The gospel message became clear to me one New Year's Eve when, after making a vow in October to stay away from my partying lifestyle, I was so bored I accepted an invitation to go to a church-sponsored New Year's Eve party. And I had fun—a *lot* of fun—all without a drop of alcohol. At midnight, when the party wound down and the pastor began his message, I was ready to listen. He spoke of starting the new year out right, with a personal relationship with Jesus Christ. Even though I'd been raised in a mainline denominational church, this time my heart truly responded.

I went home to my apartment, knelt, and confessed the mess I'd made of my life. If Jesus wanted it, he could have it.

I woke the next day a different person—one with an inability to swear, which was contrary to my normal vocabulary. I had no desire to party. I devoured the Word of God like I'd once devoured liquor. Now, forty-seven years after my salvation, a hundred Bible verses are stored in my memory.

During Bobby's second battle with cancer, I meditated on Psalm 23, focusing on the fourth verse. "Yea, though I walk through the valley of the shadow of death ..."

I kept coming back to the shadow.

Death is only a shadow, not something to be feared.

I will fear no evil.

As Bobby walked through chemo toward death, the shadow moved with me. I was deep into that dark, scary valley. But God had said his rod and his staff would comfort me. I pictured myself walking through a gloomy valley, on a path perched between a mountain wall and a deep precipice. God's rod and staff nudged me from side to side to keep me on the path so I wouldn't fall over the precipice into a crevasse.

The crevasse was the darkest despair, the kind of despair which would keep me from getting out of bed every morning. My thinking flipflopped between Psalm 23's comfort and my own denial. Bobby would get well. We would celebrate his thirtieth birthday in Disneyland. We would watch him grow old.

Or would we?

Would I be known as the mother of the boy who died?

CHAPTER 4

A BETTER PLACE

A ten-year-old boy decided to run away from home. He left his parents a note.

Mom and Dad, I'm leaving to go to a better place.

Our friend at church shared this story of finding the note from his son on the kitchen table.

Although humorous, the note could have been written by me. During the year following Bobby's diagnosis, I wanted to go somewhere else, someplace where cancer didn't exist—a warmer, better place where everyone was happy. Returning to Hawaii would have been wonderful, where we'd spent ten days with the whole family in 2008 before the sickness and unemployment. But a Hawaii trip wasn't in our future.

After healing from surgery but before starting chemo, Bobby and his wife traveled to Texas to one of the leading cancer centers in the US. They were determined to get treatment from the most cutting-edge hospital available. The doctors there did a battery of tests on him.

When they returned home to Colorado, Bobby called me.

"What are you doing back?" I expected him to be gone for a few months, not a few days.

"The doctors told me to come home and surround myself with my support system. Close friends and family."

My hand was slippery on the phone. "You mean, go home and get your affairs in order?"

"Pretty much, yeah."

Those doctors didn't know who they were dealing with. This was the *Golden Child*.

He set to work to find a doctor who would treat his cancer, in spite of the 5 percent survival rate. Bobby told me he'd be in the 5 percent, no question about it.

"We'll celebrate your complete recovery in Disneyland next year for your thirtieth birthday," I told him, hope and fear slugging it out in my heart.

After two rounds of chemo in Denver, the CT scans would show if the tumor responded. When we received the news the tumor had shrunk a little, we rejoiced. I felt as though I'd bungee jumped from a bridge. After plummeting two hundred feet down, I bounced back up, then down, then up.

***

Despite recent medical advances, the diagnosis of cancer is terrifying. We instantly bring to mind people we've known or heard about who've died after months of pain or friends and relatives whose skin turns gray and whose hair falls out. We've watched as their very life is sucked out. Cancer is like the alien monster in a sci-fi movie. We wait, holding our breath, to see what the monster will do next. Can it be killed? Or is it hiding, waiting to pounce again?

We pray for those who need healing, secretly hoping we won't ever be in the same situation. When the doctors told Bobby he'd die within six weeks without chemo, what choice did he have but to start chemo? He hoped to beat the odds. After all, he was the Golden Child.

As I watched Bobby go through gut-wrenching, cell-killing chemo, I thought about how our stomachs are made to reject foreign stuff through vomiting. Too bad he couldn't reject cancer the same way. As a mother, I wouldn't purposely feed my child poison. But there he was, submitting to the injection of liquid chemicals which burn veins, poison kidneys, kill hair follicles, and destroy cancer cells. I thought the medicine Bobby was taking would either kill him or make him better, and I'm sure at times he probably felt the same way.

★★★

When facing a diagnosis of terminal illness, you quickly discover who your true friends are. Many gather around and offer support during the first critical days of an accident or hospitalization. Meals are delivered, cards sent, flowers and gifts are brought to the hospital. Sometimes the deluge of help is overwhelming. Everyone wants to visit, to be in the know.

Like trying and failing to look away from a car accident, people want to know the details. What kind of cancer is it? What stage is it? What's the prognosis?

Then, after the initial flurry of support, life resumes, and people get busy. Many friends fall away, leaving a remnant who send cards, pray, bring a meal, clean the house, walk the dog—the myriad day-to-day responsibilities which can overwhelm a family going through a life-changing diagnosis. Chemotherapy is awful, not only for the one receiving it, but for the ones having to watch. Most people don't want to be there for the long haul.

I desperately longed to be in a different place—to get on a plane and fly far away from cancer and its devastation. But there was no way to escape my situation. My refuge would be found in the only place my heart knew to go.

My journey to that better place began by my focus on the vision at the end of the "valley of the shadow of death." I prayed through Philippians 4:6–7. "Do not be anxious about anything, but in every situation, by prayer and petition, with thanksgiving, present your requests to God. And the peace of God, which transcends all understanding, will guard your hearts and your minds in Christ Jesus" (NIV).

I threw all my anxiety over Bobby's life into the arms of Jesus.

***

The tumor in Bobby's chest stopped responding to chemo in October 2009. Could this be the end? Radiation wasn't an option. Neither was surgery, because of the location of the cancer growth. My internal roller coaster took another stomach-dropping fall.

Determined to not give up, Bobby decided to try an alternative medical clinic in Nevada. Since traditional medicine hadn't cured him, maybe something different— something radical—was called for. The roller coaster began another upward climb into hope, and my anxiety grew for something—anything—to beat the monster, no matter the cost.

The treatment would last for three weeks, five days a week. A friend of ours offered Bobby a place to stay in his two-bedroom timeshare in Lake Tahoe. We spent as much time with Bobby and Ali as we could, driving from Sacramento every weekend. Our times together were precious. We took walks, played in the snow, went to the movies, and played games. During his treatment, I'd hang out in the clinic, chatting with one of the nurses I knew from my days of living in Reno over thirty years before.

Bobby's attitude during the three weeks strengthened me. He endured eight hours of infusions every day, in addition to having to keep to a strict regimen of supplements. His diet was closely monitored and very restrictive. Yet, every time I'd see him, he was relaxed and happy. He never complained about the treatments, and he was grateful for whatever time he had left. He told me many times the quality of his life was what mattered, not the quantity. His greatest joy was to hang around his family and friends.

At the end of the three weeks, he went home, looking and feeling better than he had the prior nine months. The plan was for him to return to Reno in January for additional treatments. Excitement built to a new high. This could work! My prayers would be answered, and Bobby would live.

When I was diagnosed with cancer at the age of thirty-five, every woman who came to visit asked the same questions. *What were your symptoms? How was the cancer diagnosed?* The unspoken words were *how can I protect myself from having the same thing happen to me?*

Trying to reassure everyone exhausted me. How could it not, when cancer had struck at the heart of my faith? How could it not, when I asked those same questions?

The cancer was removed, radiation and chemo scheduled, and I was back to health within six months. Just a minor scuffle with the enemy. Nothing to worry about. A mere blip in my walk of faith with God. I hoped for the same outcome in Bobby's situation, so there would be no suffering grief upon grief. I saw a light at the end of the valley described in Psalm 23.

At that time, I had no idea my faith rested on a faulty foundation. My cancer was taken care of quickly, and I never needed to rely on God.

But after Bobby's first bout with cancer at seventeen, my foundation crumbled under the pressure of life's circumstances. I hadn't exercised the faith muscle enough to face my son's cancer diagnosis. Depression set in, and I doubted the reality of my relationship with God. I stopped going to church and did not return for a year before the Holy Spirit coaxed me back.

God tells us in his Word to be careful how we build. If our foundation is wood, hay, or stubble, the foundation will be burned up. If we build on the sand, the storms of life will wash away what we've built. Only the firm foundation of Jesus Christ will hold until the day of his return.

Everything I'd faced in my life as a Christian prepared me, without my realizing it, for the devastating loss to come. Every job loss, every betrayal by a friend, financial difficulty, health issues, internal and external pressures—all forced me to build on the one foundation which can't be destroyed.

My heart and my mind continued to battle each other for supremacy. Would the cancer kill him, or would he be victorious? I meditated on Psalm 42:11. "Why, my soul, are you downcast? Why so disturbed within me? Put your hope in God, for I will yet praise him, my Savior and my God" (NIV).

No matter the outcome, I would continue to praise God.

★★★

My father's health declined rapidly during the same year as Bobby's fight with cancer. He developed a condition called neuropathy, causing numbness in his leg muscles. Driving became more difficult, but he kept his ailment a secret. Both Mom and Dad were in their eighties, and my mom had given up her driver's license the previous year due to macular degeneration. Dad became the sole driver, taking Mom to appointments and on errands. They went out almost every day—to play bridge, to eat, to visit friends, and to shop. Once a month, they'd travel for two hours to

Reno or Tahoe to spend a few dollars in the casinos. Their traveling on the freeway concerned me. Every time they left the house, I expected to get a call from a state trooper saying they'd been in an accident.

One day, Dad and Mom returned home from running errands, and as he pulled into the garage, something happened, and he couldn't make the turn. The car bumped into the side of the garage. Mom met with Mike and me privately and asked if we'd have a conversation with Dad about not driving anymore.

I knew the conversation and its outcome would mean the end of their current way of life.

Selfishly, I thought of how difficult the solution would be for me. I'd be called upon more frequently to take my parents on errands and to do their shopping.

One more thing, Lord. How much more can I take?

Mike and I did as much as we could for them while we worked full time. We took a day off here and there to drive them up to Reno or Tahoe. We used sick time to get my parents to their numerous doctor appointments.

Every time the phone rang with my parents' number showing on the screen, a sensation like a jolt of electricity shot through me. What would it be this time? Was this the call to tell me my dad had passed away? Or he was in the hospital again?

Life's pressure cooker increased. Bobby's health was a constant ebb and flow of grief and hope. Dad's neuropathy worsened. He was in constant pain and needed to use a walker. Sometimes his legs couldn't support him, and he'd fall. Often the falls occurred in the middle of the night, and Mike would have to dash down to my parents' house to help Dad back into bed. If I was at work, Mom would call 911. I'd have to go to the hospital and sit with Mom until Dad was released. After three or four visits from the paramedics and subsequent emergency room trips, they advised my mom to seriously consider either in-home care or an alternative living situation.

Mike and I sat with Dad and had the most difficult conversation of my life, beginning with the hardest sentence of all.

"Dad, you can't live at home anymore."

We arranged to move him to a board-and-care home.

My daughter called me while we talked with the social worker in my parents' kitchen, and I walked outside to talk with her in private.

"This is harder than hearing Bobby has cancer," I told her. Telling my dad he couldn't stay home, living with his wife of sixty-five years. Telling him he had to move out, knowing he'd die someplace away from his home. Away from her.

He was eighty-nine years old.

I'd heard the term "sandwich generation," describing couples who were stuck in the middle between caring for their children and taking care of their aging parents. To me it felt more like being a grape in a wine press. The pressure increased, relentless as a pit bull planting himself for an attack.

First Corinthians 10:13 says God provides a way of escape when we feel we are pressed beyond what we can face. "No temptation has overtaken you, except such as is common to man; but God is faithful, who will not allow you to be tempted beyond what you are able, but with the temptation will also make the way of escape, that you may be able to bear it."

During those dark days, I doubted the truth of this verse. My search for "the way of escape" was desperate. Where was my better place?

By spending more and more time in prayer, I found it. My better place was within me.

★★★

When I was laid off from my well-paying job, right before Bobby's diagnosis, the economy wasn't very good for the banking business. I got another job in a different industry, at less than half my former salary and with a steep learning curve.

I took a lot of time off to spend with Bobby when he felt well enough to come to California to visit between chemo treatments. I left work early and came in late when I had to take my mom or dad to their myriad doctor appointments. As a result of all my time away from work, I was criticized by the twenty-two-member board of directors who now served as my boss.

I frequently looked to the heavens and asked, "Why me?"

Who hasn't asked the same question? We search for meaning in life's indignities.

The greater question should be, "Why not me?"

In the book of John, Jesus told his disciples, "In this world you will have trouble." My naïve assumption was I'd be immune from this kind of loss. Hadn't we already had the cancer thing in our lives? Three times? I survived cancer in the early nineties. Bobby's cancer was in remission in 1999. My dad had overcome colon cancer.

Ongoing illness, whether terminal or not, makes us vulnerable. We don't like to be vulnerable. Many times the message from the pulpit is we can conquer anything if we just have faith. "With God all things are possible." Jesus told his disciples they could move mountains if they just had faith.

If I can move a mountain, why can't I send cancer to the nether regions, ripping it out of my son's chest and casting it into the ocean?

Life should be fair. Someone else should have some of my suffering, just to equal things out.

When my kids were little, they'd argue over the smallest things. Who got the bigger cookie, whose turn it was to empty the dishwasher, who used the cool TV tray the last time. Sometimes they'd come to me and complain one or the other of them wasn't being fair.

Many times my answer to them was, "Life's not fair. Get used to it." During the times I was tempted to shake my fist at the sky and tell the Lord, "It's not fair," he brought my own words back to me.

I think a verse from the first chapter of the Old Testament's book of Job says it best.

"The Lord gave, and the Lord has taken away. Blessed be the name of the Lord."

***

God's grace gave us a reprieve after Bobby spent three weeks at the Reno clinic. God knew the storm was coming, and we needed time to breathe. The tsunami was building far out in the ocean, but God protected us from seeing it.

We celebrated Thanksgiving and Christmas with a sense of hope and gratefulness. Dad was doing well in the board-and-care home. Bobby made plans to start another business when he finished the alternative protocol. The roller coaster ride of 2009 slowed to a halt. I was grateful to get off.

I didn't get to escape to a better place physically, but I knew God had taken me to an even better place than a sunny beach in Hawaii—a deeper place of grace. Psalm 23:3 says, "He refreshes my soul" (NIV). The New King James

Version uses the word "restores" in place of "refreshes." I ended 2009 with a refreshed soul.

CHAPTER 5

ELEVEN ELEVEN—BOBBY TIME

The first time I held Bobby in my arms, I marveled at his perfection. Did Mary, the mother of Jesus, feel the same way when she held her son in the smelly barn? Did she think one day she'd watch her baby die? She must have known the Old Testament prophecies. Did she push those dark thoughts away to revel in the newborn smell of his neck, as she counted his tiny fingers and toes, as she fell deeply in love with him?

Sometimes I wonder if I would have done anything differently, had I known Bobby would die young. Perhaps I would have disciplined him less, been less strict. For sure, I'd have spent more time with him and created more memories to carry me through the years I have left until I see him again.

God's grace to me was my not knowing how short his life would be. He may have turned into a spoiled brat if I'd been easier on him. Maybe he wouldn't have committed his life to Christ.

The Bible study I attended studied Watchman Nee's book, *Changed Into His Likeness*. The chapters about Isaac were like Fourth of July fireworks in my brain.

I realized Isaac, Abraham's son, didn't do anything to inherit all his father owned. He was graced with his inheritance. He didn't have to do anything to earn it.

In the same way, when we acknowledge Jesus Christ as Lord, we receive, by grace, our inheritance. Everything Jesus has is ours. Isaac didn't walk through the property of his father and say, "I'll take this area, but not this one. I don't like that tent, so it's not part of my property." He didn't point to the herds of cattle, sheep, and goats and declare, "I only want the brown ones. The rest aren't mine."

His inheritance included slaves, some of whom may have been old or ill. Some of the parcels of land were probably barren or uninhabitable. The flocks must have included sick or injured animals. Did Isaac disregard them? No. He inherited *all* his father's belongings.

I looked at my life and realized I couldn't pick and choose which parts of God's grace I'd inherit. My heavenly Father gave me, by grace, everything in my life. Who was I to say this thing is bad or that thing is good? Nothing God gives me is bad or good—it just is.

Bobby's cancer was God's grace to me. Watchman Nee's book gives the example of Isaac, who—as Jesus trusted his Father—trusted Abraham without question, went willingly with him to Mount Moriah, and lay down on the altar as a sacrifice.

We read in James 1:17, "Every good gift and every perfect gift is from above, and comes down from the Father of lights, with whom there is no variation or shadow of turning."

It isn't my right, as a child of God, to decide whether something is good or bad.

Mary watched as her son Jesus stirred up controversy throughout Galilee. She'd probably heard rumors of plots to have him arrested and killed. Did she spend hours in prayer, begging for a miracle, asking God to show mercy and let Jesus live? Did she know in her heart the answer to her prayers would be a resounding no?

My spirit knew the cancer would kill my son. My brain, however, refused to acknowledge the fact. My brain's belief kept me going through the difficult year of pre-grief. I had to go to my job, take care of my parents, get through my daily activities.

I rejoiced with my daughter over the news of her pregnancy and prayed she'd have a boy. Somehow, in my twisted thinking, he would replace Bobby in my heart. Her baby would be the redemption of Bobby's death.

I asked God repeatedly to help me deal with the possibility of Bobby's passing. I had no idea what it would look like or how his death would change me.

∗∗∗

My memory of the year after Bobby was diagnosed is a contrast of dark and light. My work office sat in the corner of a building, with floor-to-ceiling windows on two sides. I could look out at the grassy knolls and the towering oak trees. Squirrels and birds foraged for food in the low bushes. An occasional wild turkey would wander by—to my delight. The building sat so the sun streamed in for most of the day. We must have had fewer rainy days that year because all I remember is the brightness of the sun. Every time Bobby called, I'd get up from my chair and wander back and forth in front of the windows. We'd talk about lots of things, but not how he was doing. When asked how he felt, he'd always answer, "Fine." He didn't want to talk about his illness. He just wanted to chat with his mom.

In bed at night, darkness would envelop me. Dark thoughts crept in, reminding me Bobby would die, making me stumble in my walk through the valley of the shadow of death. My mind returned again and again to the emptiness of losing my son. I tried to think about something happy, something to concentrate on to help me sleep, but nothing came. At night, I was lost in the valley with no light to guide me. There was no sunrise on the horizon. My sleep was tormented by nightmares.

When he was in high school, Bobby's curfew was eleven o'clock. I'd usually be asleep by the time he got home. He'd always come in and wake me.

"Mom, I'm home," he'd whisper, then wait for my response.

I'd crack my eye open to see the time. More often than not, it was 11:11, meaning he'd missed his curfew by eleven minutes. I'd sigh.

"Pick your battles," I'd heard from the parenting experts. So many battles during those turbulent high school years. Eleven minutes past curfew wasn't one I was ready to take on.

"Thanks, hon," I'd answer. "I love you."

"Love you too, Mom."

When Bobby left home after high school, we made a joke about 11:11. It became our special time to call or text each other. If I happened to look at the clock at 11:11, I'd call him to tell him I was thinking of him. He'd do the same thing. On November 11th, we'd race to see which one of us would call the other first. On November 11, 2009, he beat me to the call. I didn't know then it would be the last November 11th call, starting the way he started every call or every voice message.

"Mom. This is your son. Bobby."

As if I had another son. Perhaps he thought I'd forgotten his name.

I'm grateful for the memories of these special times. These are God's grace to me. Bobby's death, while tragic and painful, is part of God's inheritance. He knew before the foundation of the world I would give birth to a son who would live only thirty years—just like Jesus's mother Mary gave birth to a son who was destined to die at thirty-three. We know Jesus died to redeem sin's hold on our lives. Bobby's death was in no way noble like our Lord's, but God's plans and purposes for us are much greater than you or I can see.

Consider those beautiful hand-stitched Persian rugs. If you pull one of them close and focus on one section of threads, you can't see how they are woven together as part of the whole. You'll miss the story being told with threads if you concentrate only on a small part.

I may never see or understand our whole story until I pass through to the other side, but I know it's there waiting for me.

My nights of wandering in the valley of the shadow of death were God's grace, gently urging me to continue in prayer. His rod and staff guided me into deeper fellowship with him. He reminded me continually Bobby was in his hands, and I didn't need to worry. He'd given his heart to the Lord at a tender age—I think at three or four years old. At church family camp, he recommitted his life and was baptized. I told myself over and over he'd be in heaven if he weren't able to overcome the cancer.

***

Is there nobility in dying?

We often use the phrase, "She died after a brave battle with breast cancer," or "He battled cancer for three years before he passed." We act as if it's some noble thing to fight this illness called cancer.

The nobility lies not in the fighting, but in the person's faith and strength when faced with impending loss or death. Some face hardships with courage, others with an almost narcissistic sense of entitlement. When my dad began his slow decline into kidney failure, he complained bitterly about how terrible he felt. He was unable to find empathy in his only grandson's struggles.

I've asked myself if it's easier to lose someone suddenly or to watch them die by slow, agonizing degrees. I've come to realize loss is loss, whatever the circumstances. My dad raged against his loss of physical function and independence. I mourned for him and for my mom. I had the dual grief of watching him decline while also watching Mom's grandson Bobby grow weaker as his cancer advanced.

As human beings, we tend to compare and quantify losses—*my loss is easier/ harder/ more tragic/ less tragic than others because my child was older/ younger/ died suddenly/ died slowly.* No matter how it happens, only those who have suffered catastrophic loss understand the incredible pain which stabs your heart and steals your hope.

***

Every new day brings a reminder nothing will ever be the same. I don't need a clock's digital display to make me remember.

Mothers have their children memorized. We know their freckles, birthmarks, and personality quirks. We recognize their cry in the nursery. Mothers quickly pick out which child is theirs on a crowded soccer field.

A few months after Bobby died, the father of one of his high school friends brought over a stack of DVDs containing high school football and basketball games. Mike and I eagerly watched them, enjoying a look back at "the good old days." We easily picked Bobby out of the crowd of players, not just by the number on his back, but by the way he carried the ball, the way he ran, his subconscious gestures.

His best friend, Mark, invited us over to his home to watch a video he'd made of his trip to Colorado to visit Bobby, a year after they'd graduated from high school. Even though the images were ten years old, I loved seeing him captured in time. Mark also had a short phone video clip he'd recorded of a fishing trip. Bobby had made a joke about the size of the fish he reeled in.

One of my myriad worries was forgetting the sound of his voice if he died, but God's grace showed up yet again through these movies which I can watch any time on my computer. I can hear and see him again, just as he was when he was alive.

Any mother who has watched her child slip away knows how increasingly precious those photos and remembrances are. We cling to childhood craft projects and handwritten Mother's Day cards, loath to part with anything remotely connected to our child. Most of all, we have thousands of memories hidden in our hearts. God's grace brings us those memories, blurring the things we regret and bringing into sharp focus the memories which warm our hearts.

I'm reminded of a woman who told me her three-year-old daughter was diagnosed with a brain tumor. She was expected to live a few weeks, but this little girl survived another year and a half. They had another eighteen months of memories, family times, and holidays to treasure.

Note to file: *Good to know—sometimes doctors get it wrong.*

We talked a lot about how she did her best to keep a normal family life amid numerous trips to the emergency room. When her daughter was home, she'd hand her a dust rag. Even though she was only four years old and wheelchair-bound, her daughter knew she contributed to the family by helping dust the furniture. Those precious memories are now stored in her mother's heart, just as "eleven eleven" is stored in mine.

November 11th is no longer Veterans Day for me. It's Bobby Day.

CHAPTER 6

THE DREADED CALL

How do I tell my dad he's dying? How do I find words to deliver a death sentence to the man who raised me, loved me, and gave me confidence to try new things?

Dad and I had shared the same family practitioner for over ten years. At my annual physical, I mentioned to my doctor my dad had a follow-up appointment with him that afternoon.

"Your dad's not coming in today. Your mom canceled the appointment," the doctor told me. "His exact words were 'I'm not going.'" He explained my mom had called earlier in the morning and said my dad was too sick to come in for the follow-up.

Dad had had some kidney function tests done, and he probably knew the news wouldn't be good. I begged my doctor to tell me the test results. He put his hand on my shoulder as he delivered the news. My dad's kidneys were in the process of shutting down.

He had about two weeks to live.

I shouldn't have asked. This was the same doctor who'd told us Bobby had cancer twelve years prior.

Over dinner, my mom, Mike, and I discussed how we would tell Dad. He'd been in the board-and-care home for five months. Mike and I had been taking turns driving Mom to see Dad every day when we got home from work. We decided we'd all go together that evening.

We told Dad about his kidneys. We gently explained his time left on earth was short. The hospice nurse would visit him by the end of the week to help keep him comfortable until the end.

Dad was in denial. He kept saying, "The hospice nurse will come, and then I'll get better, right?"

"No, Dad," we'd respond. "You're not getting better."

Less than two weeks later, Mike called me from the board-and-care home. He'd taken Mom to visit, while I stayed home and cooked dinner for the three of us.

"I'm coming to get you," Mike said. "Dad can't breathe. The hospice nurse is on her way."

I turned off the oven and the stove, pulled my apron over my head, and grabbed my purse. We raced back to the board-and-care home. The hospice nurse was putting antianxiety medication under Dad's tongue as he struggled for each breath. Mom sat in the living room, tissue pressed to her eyes.

I grabbed my dad's head and yelled in his ear.

"I love you, Daddy! This is your Chickie. I hope you can hear me. You need to turn to Jesus right now. It's not too late. Turn to Jesus while you can, so we'll see you again in heaven."

Dad had previously refused to believe in the saving life of Christ. I don't know if he heard me or if my words even registered. I'll know only when I get to the other side.

He struggled for his last breath as we watched.

★★★

Bobby's last round of chemo was in January of 2010, at the alternative medical clinic in Nevada. He and Ali lost their house the same month. They couldn't continue to make house payments with no income.

Bobby came to visit us after the treatment. He was thin and pale, but his eyes were still the color of a spring sky. He was bald as a baby, and he'd even lost his eyebrows and eyelashes. We made plans to travel to Colorado to spend spring break with him. Instead, he came back to Sacramento to visit after his beloved grandpa passed away.

Bobby was in so much pain he spent the majority of the weekend curled up on the bed or lying on the couch. His weight had dropped again because eating was too painful. His pain medication also diminished his appetite. I wondered how long he'd be with us.

Two weeks later, we got the call which would change everything.

For months, I'd asked my daughter-in-law to please give me plenty of notice when Bobby got really sick. I begged her not to call me and say, "This is it." I wanted to be able to spend time with him before he died. But the message didn't come from her.

We found out about Bobby by sheer coincidence. Mike's brother and his family had been skiing near the town where Bobby lived, and they stopped in to have a pizza before driving back to Colorado Springs. They saw Ali's brother in the pizza restaurant and got up to say hello. He told them Bobby had been having trouble breathing and had gone to the hospital emergency room.

Mike's brother called us that Sunday night as I prepared for bed. "Did you know Bobby's in the hospital?"

How could Ali not have let us know? We called her cell and got voicemail. We tried Bobby's cell with the same result. We tried Ali's mom, her dad, their home phone, her brother's phones. Everyone's phone went straight to voicemail. I was frantic with worry.

Later the same evening, Ali called me in tears.

"I'm so sorry," she began. "I know I promised not to do this to you. But there's cell service in only one corner of the hospital. Every time I'd head over there to call you, someone would come and ask me for more information."

Since Bobby had never been seen at that hospital before, they ran every test known to man on him. They finally put him on oxygen and sent him home. They told him the hospice staff would be in touch.

Call family. Gather your friends. Say goodbye.

We flew to Colorado the next day. Bobby looked and acted fine when we arrived at Ali's parents' house, which was where they'd been living since they lost their home. We sat outside, enjoying a rare warm March day. No way this kid was dying.

We had dinner with Ali's family and prepared for bed in their guest room. Bobby and Ali had the entire basement apartment to themselves. The next day, Mike and Bobby went to town on some errands. Other than being rail thin, he looked fine.

By evening, he showed signs of fading. He skipped dinner and opted to partially recline on the sofa instead, where an oxygen tank blew a continuous stream of life-giving air to his lungs. He couldn't lie down because of the pressure in his chest.

By the end of the week, Heather had arrived, as well as Bobby's best friend, Mark. I let them spend as much time together as they wanted, knowing this would be their last visit.

The doctor at the hospital had told Bobby the cancer had gone crazy and had spread everywhere—into his kidneys, his liver, his lungs, his brain. All we could do was keep him comfortable and as pain-free as possible.

I drowned the guest bed with my tears. Sometimes, I felt as if I'd fill up the bedroom like a reservoir, and I'd float away on the bed. I spent every moment I could with him, sometimes sitting in a chair by his bed—just to watch him breathe.

The hardest thing during those two weeks was the emotional push-and-pull. I'd cry my eyes out upstairs in the privacy of the bedroom, anguished over his slow march toward eternity. But downstairs, sitting in the basement living room, I'd feel the peace which passes understanding.

Part of me was relieved his suffering would soon be over. He'd see Jesus face to face. He'd be free from all the pain and sin of this world.

He would be at peace.

The mom part of me sobbed in anguish over watching him slip away. I wanted to stop the progression of time, to steal back some precious moments. How would I be able to go on living without my son?

I'd climb up on the hide-a-bed next to him and hold his hand. He'd open those incredible blue eyes and focus on me for a moment.

"Hey, Mama."

"I love you, Bobby."

"I love you too, Mama." Then his eyes would close, and he'd disappear again.

When someone you love is dying, you undergo an invisible internal change. Trauma produces a lasting change—a change your heart, mind, and spirit must struggle to wrap around. Mere interruptions or events seem magnified and crushing. Decisions are overwhelming.

Life as I'd known it came to a screeching halt.

As Bobby's birthday approached, my anxiety increased. Each morning brought with it the thought, *this could be the day*.

Something in me rebelled against him dying on his birthday.

I experienced my first full-blown panic attack. I couldn't breathe. My heart pounded, and I couldn't stop crying. I called my doctor back in Sacramento, incoherently trying to tell the nurse what was happening. She called in a prescription for a low-dose antianxiety medication. The medicine relieved me enough to survive the next ten days— until Bobby was set free from his earthbound life to live a greater one with God.

***

I read somewhere practice prepares the mind, but suffering prepares the heart. I'd barely had time to grieve my father's passing. Now, I sat watching my son slip away. My heart was certainly being prepared, but I didn't know for what.

I wondered if it would be easier if we'd gotten a call that he'd died suddenly. Which is easier—to lose your child slowly, dreadfully—or to answer the door to two police officers who tell you there was a car accident or a gang shooting? It's the difference between a surgeon's quick cut with a sharp instrument and a slow walk through a bed of coals.

I met a woman who'd lived in what was considered a bad part of Sacramento. Gangs were everywhere, and they openly encouraged her son to join them. Afraid of losing her child to a gang, she moved the family to another area of town with a new school and a new environment. As it turns out, gang activity had reached that neighborhood too. Her son became the victim of a drive-by shooting while standing on his own porch.

Guarding our children from harm is our job as mothers and fathers. If we can't keep our children from evil, we must be bad parents. Guilt is crushing, no matter if your child is two or twenty-two. The truth is, we're powerless to keep them totally safe.

When they're babies, we tuck them in at night, and we know where they are at all times. As they grow, however, their circle widens, and our influence and control shrinks. We have to hold them with open hands, trusting God.

When our child dies, our choice is to either hate God and blame him because we think he's cruel, or trust him, even though we don't understand. Even though the hurt presses into our heart like a hot iron. Even though we think about joining our son or daughter in death, because to go on living without them is unbearable.

The call from my daughter-in-law from the hospital emergency room had felt the same as falling into a thorn bush. Every movement cut and sliced while reality tightened its grip. A thousand barbs pierced deep into flesh.

Somehow God's grace sustained me on that journey to Colorado. He gently held my bleeding heart so I could make the last trip to see my son. Mike and I had sat together, holding hands silently, as reality smacked us with the full force of a boxer's knockout punch.

If Bobby's life were a novel, the tension would ratchet up, the odds against him would increase, but something would happen at the end to make everything turn out all right. As the hero, he'd have a life-changing moment.

Perhaps it would be discovered he didn't really have cancer, but a rare disease which was curable, like in the television show *House*. Or a faith healer would pray for him, and he'd turn the corner and begin to get well, after some inner revelation of why he'd gotten cancer in the first place. Perhaps there would be a malpractice suit and a huge insurance settlement—anything which would make sense in fiction's make-believe world.

But this was real life. As real as it gets. The monster couldn't be killed, and Bobby was its victim. Everyone else stood by, powerless. Our only hope was in the reality of eternity.

If God is good, then I had to believe Bobby's life—and his death—had a plan and a purpose. As painful as it was to face the death of my child, I chose to accept God's choice and rest in God's grace.

CHAPTER 7

SELF-SUFFICIENCY IS NOT MY GOD

If you're the mother of a son, don't ever stop touching him. When he's little, he's easy to snuggle, to cuddle, and kiss. Then, they grow into prickly teenagers and into men—and touching, kissing, hugging, and stroking the arm of your grown son can feel strange.

Deep down inside, they don't mind. They secretly still like being cuddled by their mom.

I spent many hours in that basement apartment, watching and waiting. Sometimes, I'd climb up onto the sofa bed and sit as close to Bobby as I could. He'd wake up for a moment, then drape his arm over my leg. I enjoyed the luxury of being able to hold his hand and stroke his head.

As the days wore on, he looked more and more like a ninety-year-old man. His thirtieth birthday came and went without celebration, except inside my heart. I rejoiced at the thought I'd given birth to such a kind and generous man.

The day he started on oral morphine, he gathered his closest friends and family around. He told us he had something to say. He began by telling each of us how much he loved us and how we'd enriched his life.

Then, just before the hospice nurse administered the drug, he said, "Wouldn't it be a bummer if this wasn't the real deal? I would've wasted your time."

We all cracked up in the midst of our tears.

His body shrank day by day as he stopped eating. Everyone pitched in, trying to comfort him. Ali's brother got some lotion and rubbed Bobby's feet. Her other brother lay on the bed next to him and stroked his arm and his head. My heart squeezed, watching as these two manly men were reduced to tenderness.

Sometimes, I'd nudge him awake. His eyes would open, brilliant blue and full of life.

"Hi, Mama," he'd say. "I love you." As soon as his eyes closed again, he'd return to the look of an old man.

A few days before he died, he gathered the family again to give hugs, kisses, and goodbyes.

"I'm so tired. I'm ready to go." His labored breathing made talking difficult.

Everything stopped. We sat by his bedside for several hours, waiting. This is how I wanted him to go, quiet and peaceful.

Then life crowded back in again. Bobby's nieces and nephews needed to be fed, snow had to be shoveled, and dogs had to be let out for a run.

Mike, Ali, and I stayed, still watching, waiting.

In a moment of wakefulness, Bobby asked, "Are you going to wait for the hammer to fall?"

"What do you mean?"

"For me to die?"

"As long as it takes," I responded in a voice thick with unshed tears.

★★★

I discovered, through Bobby's illness, places deep inside me needing safety. I'd bought into the American culture of creating a false sense of security through my abilities, my income, my home. We take comfort in the idea if we save enough for retirement, we'll somehow be safe. Safe from what? We don't know!

Death forces us to look at how we view life. In 1 Corinthians 15:55, Paul says, "Where, O death, is your victory? Where, O death, is your sting?" (NIV). No one is safe from death, whether from natural causes in old age or from a terminal diagnosis or a fatal car accident.

As the world continues to find ways to stay young and live longer, many Christians fall into the same mindset. Watching Bobby slipping closer and closer to eternity, I realized what Paul said in 1 Thessalonians 4:13 is true. "Brothers and sisters, we do not want you to be uninformed about those who sleep in death, so that you do not grieve like the rest of mankind, who have no hope" (NIV). I knew I'd see Bobby again and be with him for all eternity. He'd be healed, free from pain, free from ever getting cancer again.

There would be days and months of sorrow, but I felt peace, knowing Bobby's days had been written in the Lamb's book of life. I just didn't understand why the number of his days was less than mine, though I asked God many times.

Why?

He didn't answer.

★★★

In grief, there is no right or wrong and no rules in death and dying. That's why we could laugh over Bobby's antics when he was drugged up with morphine and cry at the same time over our impending loss of his presence.

One evening, a couple of the guys were talking about fixing up their old Land Rover, not realizing Bobby was listening. They joked about making it really loud like their cousin's old Jeep.

Bobby opened his eyes and added his two cents, in drawn-out words as he struggled for breath. "If you do, I'm going to ask God to resurrect me, so I can come back and haunt you."

He fell back on the pillows, exhausted, but we laughed until we cried.

How many tears could I cry until I was dry?

People die the same way they lived. Bobby's terminal diagnosis gave him a chance to tell his inner circle how much they meant to him. He expressed how each one enriched his life. He told humorous stories about each person and made each one of us feel special. I knew, as did everyone else, what was most important to Bobby—family, good friends, God, and the beauty of his creation.

***

I learned a lot about patience waiting for Bobby to die. There was no way to control the situation. My stress would have been relieved by knowing when his death would happen, but it was up to God to name the day and the hour.

Human nature tells us we should always be doing something or going somewhere. But death has a way of throwing a stick in the spokes. My life not only crashed to a halt, but also narrowed down to one activity—spending as much time as possible with my son. That meant being in the room with him, watching him breathe. It meant sitting beside him, reading, stroking his arm.

My spirit became still as I entered into his suffering.

I'd like to think I gained wisdom in those hours. This experience became a part of me and altered me so profoundly I could never go back to the way I'd been. There's a line in the movie *As Good as It Gets*, where Jack Nicholson's character says, "You make me want to be a better man." Watching Bobby live and die made me want to be a better person.

We'd had many talks about his life after death. He had a calm assurance of his eternal destiny. He repeatedly told me his life was about quality, not quantity. The Bible says in Philippians 1:21, "For to me, to live is Christ and to die is gain" (NIV). I'd heard the verse many times in my Christian walk. Bobby made it real to me. He knew his death would be only the beginning of a different kind of life.

I'd spent much of my life trying to achieve something out there in the world which would give me significance. I thought if I raised my kids up to be good adults, I'd find everlasting satisfaction. Then it was my goal to make a hundred thousand dollars a year. When I achieved that, I asked myself, "Is this all there is?"

I didn't get satisfaction. Rather, I felt trapped in a job I hated. Maybe if I had a certain kind of car, it would give me the satisfaction I craved. My needs and wants were all tied up in things having nothing to do with Jesus.

The writer of Ecclesiastes said it best. "Then I looked on all the works that my hands had done And on the labor in which I had toiled; and indeed all was vanity and grasping for the wind. There was no profit under the sun" (Ecclesiastes 2:11).

★★★

Death has a way of stripping us down to the barest elements. Watching my son die put me in touch with myself and made me confront my core values. I'd always valued control and self-sufficiency over everything, but the one most important core value is not found in anything our present world values.

The one thing, the only thing, is the Person in whom you put your trust.

God held me as I cried. He listened to me wail over my son's suffering. He knew what it was like to watch a son die.

The Bible tells us God is able to empathize with us in our suffering. Hebrews 4:15 says it this way: "For we do not have a High Priest who cannot sympathize with our weaknesses." He tells us to comfort others with the comfort we have received.

The prophet Jeremiah says in chapter 8, "I would comfort myself in sorrow; my heart is faint in me" (v.18 NIV). My heart was certainly faint. How would I survive after he was gone?

One day Bobby caught me crying as I watched him sleep. He reached for me and grabbed my hand. "Don't cry, Mama."

"I'm going to miss you so much," I sobbed.

"I'm sorry," he responded.

He was apologizing to me! What an extraordinary young man I had raised.

"I'm sorry if I'm not doing it right," he added.

I wasn't sure what he meant. Maybe it was the morphine talking. Stroking his arm, I said, "You're doing fine." He smiled, and then, his eyes closed again.

Every activity in the house revolved around Bobby and his condition during those last days. He was the focus of our attention. He would have hated it if he'd been aware someone was always with him. He loved being part of a tightknit family group but never being the center of attention.

At any gathering, he'd skirt around the edges and throw out witty comments designed to get a chuckle. His cutting sense of humor was part of his charm. He never directed his sarcasm to someone who couldn't take it. He treated the outcast tenderly, often drawing someone into his inner circle who others considered strange or geeky. Bobby was the cool guy who everyone wanted to be like.

When he was in high school, there was a kid on his basketball team who was socially awkward. The popular clique shunned him, even though his basketball skills were stellar. Bobby made it a point to befriend the kid, which instantly elevated the young man's social standing in the high school.

Most high school yearbooks have a "Most Likely To ..." section. Some of the headings are "Most likely to start a software company," and "Most likely to become president." No one would have ever conceived Bobby's heading would be "Most likely to die of cancer at the age of thirty." His would have been "Most likely to become an NBA star," or "Most likely to become a millionaire."

Instead, he was content to excel in his business, hang out with family, and backpack in the wilderness. The things he held dear were evident in the way he lived his life.

I had hours of time to meditate on the way he lived and the way he was dying. He desired to leave this world surrounded by family and close friends. His was a heart at peace, both with his life and with his eternal destiny.

How could I not learn from this life lesson? God's grace lifted me up and set me in a place where my sufficiency came from him. My need for control shrank as the cross became magnified. I stopped asking the *why* question and began giving thanks for what he was doing, even as I sat in the basement—watching, waiting.

Even as I wondered every day if this would be the day Bobby would step into glory.

CHAPTER 8

THE LAST BREATH

My Golden Child took his last breath ten days after his thirtieth birthday. The family gathered around, watching him struggle to breathe. The hospice nurse hovered in the background, tears streaming down her cheeks. She'd told us her job was more difficult when her patient was young.

And then, quiet as a sigh, my Golden Child was gone.

The minutes after he stopped breathing are a blur. The only thing I remember is being alone in the room with him. I crawled up onto the hide-a-bed where he sat, his head resting against the back of the sofa. I don't know how long I sat with him, kissing his cheek and stroking his arm. Mike touched me gently on the shoulder and told me it would be best to go upstairs. He didn't want me to see the men from the funeral home put him in a bag to take him away. I cried as I pried myself away, knowing I'd never see him again in the flesh.

I'd spent the previous two and a half weeks waiting for this moment, and now I was torn between screaming and running into a closet and gathering him in my arms one last time.

The pain of watching him die had ended, but a new and forever pain had begun. I couldn't stop crying.

Practice prepares the mind, but suffering prepares the heart.

I didn't know then what my heart was prepared for. I would discover that later in the long months which followed.

***

I wrote in my journal I felt as if I had a wound, and I wanted to keep stabbing it. I didn't want to forget Bobby for even an instant. Constantly reminding myself he was gone would ensure he'd remain alive in my memory. I was desperately afraid of forgetting something about him—the way he felt, the way he smelled, the color of his eyes, his voice.

In my struggle to make sense of his death, I wanted to somehow redeem what had happened. I became focused on becoming a different person, as if I could change by my own will. I wanted others to say, "Jane, you're so much more loving these days," or "You're so compassionate."

Then my answer could be, "Well, it wasn't until my son's death when I became more loving and compassionate." Bobby's death needed to mean something. I didn't want him to have died in vain. My mind needed an answer to the *why* question.

Bobby died so I could be a better person.

When someone dies, there's an urgency to do something, get involved in a cause, form a foundation in the person's name. Some people get involved in an activity to help them deal with the pain. Mothers Against Drunk Driving began because of a child killed by a drunk driver. Amber Alerts started because a child was abducted. Parents need to feel their child's death should count for something, or perhaps could help others prevent the same tragedy.

I spoke with a woman whose little girl died from a brain tumor. Her healing began when she went to the local high school and asked to work with handicapped teens. Another mom I know delivers care packages to families who have lost a child. I wanted to start a fundraising effort for sarcoma research, but I couldn't dredge up the energy.

The reality is death deprived me of control. My carefully detailed plan for my life didn't include my son dying before me. My life and my expectations had blown up in my face. I lost the feeling of invulnerability I thought was mine because of my faith. Romans 8:28 tells us, "And we know that in all things God works for the good of those who love him, who have been called according to his purpose" (NIV).

How could this event, this loss, this personal tragedy possibly work for my good?

My Bible study group was working through the book, *Abide in Christ*, by Andrew Murray. In the chapter on affliction and trial, Murray tells us to "be much with Him alone. Beware of the comfort and distractions friends so often bring. Let Jesus Christ Himself be your chief companion and comforter." My journal became a way for me to pour out all my heartache and grief to God as I spent time alone with him. Thus began a moment-by-moment abiding and surrendering.

Something Bobby told me stuck in my mind after he died. He'd said the purpose of his life was to glorify God. Looking back, I see even though he knew he was dying, he never said, "This isn't fair." He never whimpered or complained about the pain. He wanted to spend his last days and hours surrounded by those he loved.

★★★

When your child dies, there is a tearing of your heart. I picture it like trying to separate two pieces of paper which have been glued together.

When your spouse dies, you become a widow or widower. When both of your parents are gone, you become an orphan, no matter what your age. There isn't a word for a parent whose child has died. There should be some sort of sign for grieving parents to wear so we can recognize each other. There's an instant connection, an aha moment. They've been there. They know.

During the first few months after his death, I clung tightly to the hope I'd see Bobby again in heaven. Living on the earth seemed pointless. People rushed to buy the latest electronic gadget or to dress in the latest fashion, trying to fit in and to do things right.

Without Jesus, I would have been tempted to end my life. What would be the purpose of living?

We are to glorify God in every circumstance. If we concentrate on that, it becomes more about the glorification and less about the circumstance. Some circumstances we call good, and some we call bad. In my moment-by-moment abiding, I leaned into Jesus's arms so I could truly glorify him and forget about the awful truth—Bobby was gone from my sight.

Some days I was angry with him for dying. How dare he leave me in so much pain? It was his fault I cried every day. Every memory of him was like salt poured into an open wound. Everything I saw, every song on the radio, reminded me of him. Sometimes grief hit me like a sucker punch in the gut, ambushing me if I dared forget about him for a few minutes.

Grief is lonely, the solitary drip of a leaky faucet. Unlike its brothers, the raindrops on the window on a stormy night, it drips alone.

Grief sneaks up on you, grabs you from behind, and makes you cry.

There's a part of the heart which hurts so badly it goes into a kind of shock, like a person who's injured in an accident but feels no pain. Eventually the adrenaline from the accident wears off, and the body feels again. The heart is similar.

The pain-shock-pain-healing process pushed me to look to Jesus for balm. My comfort came from telling myself when I died, I'd get to see Bobby again. I lamented over the number of years I'd have to wait. My dad died at eighty-nine, and my mom was still active at eighty-six. If I continued to be healthy, I'd have another thirty-plus years of living without my son.

I remember vividly something God revealed to my heart. As I repeated my mantra of getting to see Bobby again in heaven, God told me my hope for heaven was that I'd see *his* Son. Like a splash of cold water, I realized my life is to glorify God, not to glorify Bobby.

***

There's a secret club made up of parents who have lost children to death— the worst kind of tragedy a parent can face. It is a club whose rules are understood only by the members, with a secret language nonmembers don't get.

Those on the outside cannot understand the irrevocable, lifelong pain which membership in this club brings. In their ignorance, they often judge us.

"Move on. Get over it. Get on with your life."

That's like telling an amputee to get over the loss of a limb—impossible to get over, but definitely possible to live with. When I faced judgment from others over how I handled my grief, I could choose to become angry and shut the other person out or take the grace I'd been given through Bobby's death and love them—one of the most difficult lessons I learned. Others could relate only because of their loss, not mine—a job loss, the death of a beloved pet, or temporary loss of mobility from a car accident. When others wanted to compare their loss to mine, I struggled to find grace.

When I look back at how I wanted to be a better person because of his death, I see the work God has done in me. I've become much closer to God, my Father, and Jesus, my brother. They comfort me in the way I need to be comforted. In his book, *Abide in Christ*, Andrew Murray warns us not to become too dependent on the comfort of others. They disappoint. They don't always come through. Sometimes, they keep us in a place of depression when God is calling us to walk in victory. "But I do not want you to be ignorant, brethren, concerning those who have fallen asleep, lest you sorrow as others who have no hope" (1 Thessalonians 4:13).

Part of the process of grieving is to realize our lives also are finite, just as our loved one's was. We come face to face with our own mortality, and it's frightening. Everything we believe in is questioned.

"Is there really a heaven?"

"Am I really saved? Will I go to heaven?"

"Is there a God?"

God allowed me to ask the hard questions. I read the popular books of the day, *Ninety Minutes in Heaven* and *Heaven Is For Real*. I searched for some comforting reassurance Bobby wasn't alone. I obsessed over the thought of him being lonely. I brought to mind those who we'd known who had died. I prayed there was a "greeting committee" of familiar faces to show Bobby around. I didn't want him to be sad. My own sadness was enough for both of us.

In the exhaustion of grief, my brain was frozen. I felt as if I'd stumbled into a thick blanket of fog. Decisions needed to be made, but I couldn't concentrate. I returned to work less than a week after Bobby died. I'd already been gone for three weeks. I don't know how I functioned for those two weeks—until we had to return to Colorado for the memorial service.

***

Parents who have experienced the devastating loss of a child try to return to normal, but there is no longer a "normal." Life will never be the same.

I thought I'd cried myself dry during the two and a half weeks we spent watching Bobby slip away. When we returned home, my tears didn't stop. I cried every day. My first thought upon waking was *he's gone.* I'd weep into my morning tea, then get ready to go to work. At night, Mike and I would hold each other in bed and cry over our loss. Sometimes, I'd dream about Bobby, and I'd wake up wracked with sobs.

I found myself constantly on guard for sad songs on the radio. There were a few songs that reminded me of him. If one came on during my ride to or from work, I'd jam my finger onto the button to change stations. I couldn't bear to look at the clock at 11:11. If it was 11:10, I'd force myself to look away until 11:12. Reminders of him were everywhere.

I remember giving myself permission to put aside my grief for one day. One day to let my wound rest. One day when I wouldn't pick off the scab. One day to receive strength to continue.

We returned to Colorado for the memorial service. It snowed that April morning, and the driveway of Mike's brother's house had to be cleared before we could back out of the driveway. Our rental car slid and skidded down the icy road. I was sick with worry and dread. What if we crashed the car and couldn't get to the service in time? What if I missed my son's funeral?

When we arrived at the chapel, I sat in the front row, barely able to greet the friends and family who had flown from Sacramento to be there. I stared at the program.

No parent—especially no mother—should have to read their child's funeral program.

This is what it said:

Psalm 37:16—A little that a righteous man has is better than the riches of many wicked.

A dear friend used this Psalm to describe how he felt about the short time we all had with Robert, and I could not agree more. Robert desired all of us to focus on who he was today, to meditate on the strength and courage he gained from God, and the fact that we would all have the opportunity to see him again very soon. So, I thank you so much for being a part of this day as we all strive to do that for a man that meant so much to so many.

The reception after the service is a blur. I know I met most of the over two hundred people who attended, but their names and faces washed away in my tears. Many had written notes and stories of what Bobby had meant to them. These were displayed on posters around the room. A video montage of photos from Bobby's birth through his death played on a big screen television in one corner. Everyone wanted to tell me what a special man Bobby was. When I couldn't take any more, Mike and I drove to his brother's house where our family was gathered.

What a relief to kick off my shoes and be welcomed into the loving arms of my dear ones. A couple of the cousins shared stories about their antics with Bobby and Heather. I heard an unfamiliar sound and realized it was the sound of my own laughter.

How could I laugh on the day we memorialized my son's death? What kind of a mother was I?

When I got home, I made an appointment to talk to a Christian counselor.

"I'm not handling this very well," I told her.

"How do you think you should be handling it?"

I had no answer. I wanted her to tell me the correct way to grieve. As if there were a formula. Or a list to follow. I thought if I could just follow a set of rules, I'd get through the next few months of bereavement.

With words of encouragement, she explained there is no correct or proper way to grieve. I had been looking at others, thinking they were judging me. I was so preoccupied with what others thought, I didn't let myself show emotion. I assumed if I left work early because I couldn't handle the stress, they would take it as a sign of weakness on my part. I thought if someone came to my office and found me crying, they'd think I wasn't fit for my position of leadership.

One of my board members came to me and gave me permission to do whatever I had to do to get through the next months. By contrast, some of the other board members complained behind my back that I wasn't functioning at a hundred percent, or even 75 percent.

I relied heavily on God's grace for others during this time. Instead of lashing out, I grieved in private and struggled to bring a spirit of forgiveness with me to work.

I still struggle over the real and implied judgment of others on how I handled Bobby's death.

I asked a friend for the phone number of someone else who was grieving over her son, a son who'd died three months prior to Bobby. The friend wouldn't pass along her phone number. She didn't want me to "wallow" with the other woman. She felt I'd pull the other woman further down into a dark place. I just wanted someone to grieve with, someone who knew what it was like. Instead, I received a stiff arm in the face.

Back off, was the message.

It was time to find healing in a different place.

CHAPTER 9

GRIEF SHARE AND SHARING GRIEF

Most Christians have a church where they go on Sunday, and I'm no different. My husband and I are involved in a small home group, and we attend Sunday school classes. It's the best way to get to know others and to make friends, especially if one attends a large church as we do.

Previously, we'd gone to the same small fellowship for twelve years. We knew the other families and their struggles. Our church placed a high value on turning to God in times of suffering and trial and to not hold back anything the Lord wanted to do during the process.

I openly shared my pain with my sisters in our Bible study. I was criticized.

"Where is your victory?" they asked. "We need to see you are turning this over to God and allowing him to give you victory." I gradually withdrew from the group, which caused more criticism. According to them, I wasn't grieving correctly.

In 1969, Elizabeth Kubler Ross wrote what many consider the definitive book on death. In her classic book, *On Death and Dying*, she theorizes grief has five stages—denial, anger, bargaining, depression, and acceptance.

I spent part of my time in the anger stage—angry with Bobby for dying, angry I had to get up every day and go to work, impatient with others when they didn't remember my loss. I was especially angry when my church fellowship didn't understand what I was going through. I struggled just to get out of bed.

In times past, when a woman lost her husband, she'd don widow's weeds for a year. Society dictated she seclude herself in her home without social contact during her year of mourning. After the twelve months, she could once again join in fellowship. She could wear bright colors again.

During the months following Bobby's death, I wished I had a sign to wear—to indicate to others I was grieving. Or a jagged cut on my cheek with thick black stitches. People would look at it and say, "Wow. That must hurt!" Explaining the cut on my cheek would be easier than trying to explain why I was sad, depressed, grouchy, tearful, or touchy.

I thought about inventing a series of buttons to wear. Red would mean *No! Do not approach! Don't ask me how I'm doing, or I'll be forced to lie and say "Fine."*

Yellow would mean *Approach with Caution. I'm barely making it today, so a pat on the shoulder would be appreciated.*

A green button would mean *All clear. I'm okay and I'm functioning. I may actually tell a joke. But if I hear the song on the radio, all bets are off.*

My study through Andrew Murray's *Abide in Christ* helped me realize through Jesus's crucifixion I'm able to have the same life as Christ—the surrender of self-will, the denial of flesh, separation from the world, and losing my life to find it in him. And I had his continued guidance, with his rod and staff, through the darkness of the valley of the shadow of death.

My husband and I joined a Grief Share group where—at last!—we found kindred spirits. People were willing to talk about their loss in a warm, caring environment. The wound in my heart began to heal as I offered hope to my fellow sufferers.

★★★

Imagine going to the dentist to have a cavity filled. The dentist drills out all the old, decayed parts of the tooth. Halfway through, he stops. "Do you want to take a break?"

Your jaw aches. You're tired of the sound of the drill. You can take the break or not, but you can't stop altogether. At some point, the tooth decay will have to be dug out. Going through grief was, for me, like that tooth. All my feelings had to be dug out before I could heal. Anything left inside would fester.

My feelings, shoved down during the year after Bobby was first diagnosed, rose to the surface, and I cried even more easily than before. Melancholy crept in, like a tide rushing in and rising higher and higher before receding. Other times despondency was a soft surf lapping at my feet. As the months progressed, grief became less of an engulfing tidal wave and more of a steady ache.

I felt letting go of sadness would somehow diminish Bobby's impact on my life, as though he'd become less important to me if I could get along without him. Going without thinking about him for several hours was always a surprise. Then grief would ambush me—the sniper in the weeds, always waiting to take me down.

Being alive means moving forward, like a people-mover at the airport. I wished for an emergency shut-off switch. I didn't want to move forward, but rather to stand still and let the rest of the world pass by. I feared moving forward would take me farther and farther away from Bobby, until I couldn't see him anymore.

Little by little I inched toward what I call my "watershed moment" when Bobby's death wasn't my last thought before sleep and my first thought when my eyes opened in the morning.

My solace had been in picturing Bobby in heaven with all the people we've known who have died, comforted to know he wasn't alone or lonely. But then the realization struck—when I finally reached heaven, the reunion would not be like an earthly one, a bittersweet greeting, as in "I've missed you so much!"

That future meeting will be like being reunited with part of my body. My focus will be on Christ, not on others. My reunion won't be sad. Not "There's my son! There's Bobby!" I will see him perfect, in spirit, but as a brother in Christ, not as my son.

My focus will be on Jesus.

That's why I could eventually say thanks be to God he removed the fear of death. Hebrews 2:14–15 says, "Inasmuch then as the children have partaken of flesh and blood, He Himself likewise shared in the same, that through death He might destroy him who had the power of death, that is, the devil, and release those who through fear of death were all their lifetime subject to bondage."

But the battle wasn't over.

I had dinner one evening a few months after Bobby died with a couple of friends from work. One of the women, trying to be comforting, said, "He's in a better place."

Anger rose up in me so strong, I wanted to snap an acid-filled response. "How could he be in a place better than with me?"

My mood turned sullen for the remainder of the meal. I decided I would never have anything to do with the woman again.

★★★

The anger phase of grief can be deadly for relationships. I'm grateful for God's grace keeping Mike and me in sync while we both grieved for our son. An acquaintance shared with me she and her husband divorced because of their child's death. Her husband couldn't express his grief and refused to acknowledge his pain. She wanted to talk about their child and remember her antics, but he wouldn't let himself go there. Communication ground to a halt, eventually destroying their marriage.

By contrast, another woman and her husband who unexpectedly lost a daughter now have a thriving worship ministry. They grieve together and support each other as the pain ebbs and flows.

My entry into the secret club of mothers who have lost children has brought me into fellowship with some amazing women of faith. I expected to see women broken by the worst possible circumstance. Instead, I found women who are compassionate, caring, and doing things they would have never done had they not lost a child. They are women who trust God so completely, they can't be moved. They've faced the shadow monster of death and survived.

My friend Tammy wrote an amazing book about her son's tragic death. *Gone in an Instant: Losing My Son, Loving His Killer* talks about her triumph over grief by learning to forgive the young man who murdered her son.

I wanted to be one of those women, but until I went to Grief Share, I had my doubts about getting to that point. At Grief Share, we heard stories of a woman whose son had died in a drive-by gang shooting, one whose son was killed by a drunk driver, and one whose daughter committed suicide by overdosing on drugs. My circumstance seemed small in comparison to their loss. I'd had a year to prepare for Bobby's death. Their children's sudden deaths took them by surprise.

Sharing my story and how far I'd come since then was healing for me. I'd lived in the valley of the shadow of death a terribly long time, and now, I was slowly being guided by God into the light.

"He leads me beside still waters. He restores my soul" (Psalm 23:2–3). This is the part of the psalm I'd been missing. In his book, *A Shepherd Looks at Psalm 23*, W. Phillip Keller talks about the fragility of life, about its unpredictability and perils. We can live in anxiety and fear or in rest and faith in our heavenly Shepherd.

I remember having coffee with a coworker, and he asked me what I'd learned from my son's death. An odd question, to be sure, but after a moment's thought, I said, "I've learned that nothing in this life is certain. Tragedy happens when we least expect it."

But Psalm 23 reminds us we walk *through* the valley of the shadow. We don't stop and live there, nor do we die there. Through all the circumstances I face in life, God continually restores my soul—if I allow him full rein.

I had a vivid dream several months after Bobby's death. I'd been attending Grief Share and was learning much about the grieving process. In my dream, I was swimming in a lake. A few feet away, Bobby's head popped up out of the water.

"Hey, Mama!"

His head was bald, as if he'd recently completed chemo.

I swam over to him and embraced him. Just as I grabbed onto him, he started to sink. Down, down he went, under the murky water. All I could do was hold his hand. I pulled as hard as I could to bring him back up to the surface, but he kept sinking. Finally, I had to let go in order to breathe.

I told the dream to my husband for his opinion. My husband's middle name should be Joseph, from the Old Testament story of Jacob's twelve sons. Joseph, one of the two sons of Jacob and Rachel, was gifted at interpreting dreams, and during his captivity in Egypt, became Pharoah's right hand because he could interpret Pharoah's disturbing nightmares.

Like Pharaoh with Joseph, whenever I have what seems to be a spiritually inspired dream, I tell my husband. And like the biblical Joseph, he's spot-on 99 percent of the time.

This time, all he said was, "You're learning to let Bobby go."

Was it all right to let him go? I stumbled upon one of my journal entries from October of 2010:

What kind of a mother am I? It's only been seven months, and I haven't thought about him all day.

My friends at Grief Share assured me it was all right not to think of him every moment. There must have been stretches of time before Bobby was diagnosed when I didn't think of him for several days. He lived a few thousand miles away and had his own life. That's why those 11:11 texts were so special to me. The texts meant in spite of our distance, he thought of me.

As I learned about bereavement, God lavished his grace on me to help me heal. I wept with others at our Grief Share group. I found snippets of encouragement in books and brought them to the group. Comforting Scripture passages came alive in new ways, and I shared them with those who were still stuck in a quagmire of deep, seemingly endless sorrow.

I felt a little guilty for my whole year with Bobby—a year to say goodbye and to spend as much time as possible with him. Others in the group, those whose loved ones had suffered sudden death, hadn't had such a blessing. Some dropped out of the group, not ready to openly grieve. In fact, Mike and I had started attending another Grief Share group shortly after Bobby's and Dad's deaths. We were overwhelmed. It was too soon. We needed extra time to process what had happened, so we signed up to attend the next cycle.

Sometimes, people just need more time to make the long walk from pain to peace.

***

I talked to a friend the other day whose cousin died a year ago. My friend thought her aunt's continuing posting on his Facebook page every night wasn't healthy. I told her to let it go. Facebook posting was her aunt's way of coping. If she persisted for, say, another year, it might be time then to have a talk with her.

I called Bobby's cell phone for a couple of weeks, just to hear his voice, but that ended when his wife discontinued his number.

Everyone has to deal with grief in their own way. There's no right or wrong way to express the loss of a loved one, especially when a child is lost. Some clean the child's room out right away, perhaps to avoid the memories. Other parents leave their child's bedroom exactly the same for months—even years.

It took nine years before I got rid of anything remotely connected to Bobby. Old notes, craft projects, school papers—all of them were stored in my cedar chest, along with one of his favorite shirts. The day he died, Ali asked if there was anything of Bobby's I wanted. I sobbed as I asked if I could have one of his T-shirts. He loved a certain brand and wore it exclusively. She opened his dresser drawer and told me to pick one.

I grabbed the one on top. Not until months later did I realize the chosen shirt was the same shirt he'd worn in our family photo in Hawaii, taken just a few months before he got sick.

CHAPTER 10

TIME HEALS ALL WOUNDS

"Are you ready for the holidays?"

Needles pierced my heart every time someone asked the question. Who wants to celebrate Thanksgiving, Christmas, or New Year's when they're still grieving? I wanted to sleep through the entire season. If I could wake up on the other side of January, everything would be better. What could we find to celebrate, anyway? Both Bobby and my dad were gone, and our daughter-in-law had broken off contact with us. She needed to move on, she told us.

Move on?

Without us?

Had our relationship been a lie? Did she only pretend to love me because of my son? Now he was gone, was she free to end the charade?

I'd lost my son *and* my adopted daughter. Bitterness wrapped its tendrils around me and squeezed my life.

I continued to text her every week, determined to win her back. I wanted—no, I needed to have her enter into my grief. I'd lost so much already and couldn't face another loss.

We were like a divorcing couple. One spouse wants to make the marriage work, but the other one wants out. The more one pushes, the farther away the other pulls. The one left behind is in denial.

How can you leave me? What have I done? Don't you love me?

Abandonment crushed my spirit. I longed for a relationship which had clearly ended with her letter to me, stating in plain English we were through. I was embarrassed to tell others my daughter-in-law wanted nothing to do with me. I must have done something so terrible she couldn't forgive me. I examined every word I'd said during Bobby's last days, trying to find any innocent remark which could have been taken wrong. Had I criticized her caretaking? Did she feel I blamed her in some way for his death?

Like a wife whose husband has left her, I checked my email every day, hoping against hope she'd relent.

★★★

As parents, we tend to take the blame when something happens to our children. If they fall off the monkey bars and break an arm, we say, *I shouldn't have let him climb so high.* A teenager has a car accident? *I shouldn't have let her drive so soon.* We take very seriously the responsibility given to us by God.

When Bobby got cancer the first time, I blamed myself. When he got cancer the second time, I racked my brain to see if there was anything we could have done to prevent the recurrence of the disease. Should we have made him eat better? Maybe we shouldn't have allowed him to have such an aggressive radiation treatment at seventeen. Could we have done something to prevent him from dying?

As parents, we cling to any tiny thread which would help explain why this tragedy happened.

As Christmas approached, I let a few friends get a glimpse of my suffering. I craved sympathy. There's a kind of notoriety in grieving. When you've lost a child, you get a golden ticket out of a lot of things. You can use it for many excuses. I used mine to avoid entering into the joy of Christ's birth.

The flesh loves our indulgence in pity, wanting the attention of others. If I mentioned why I wasn't up to celebrating Christmas, the response was immediate.

"Oh, of course. I'm sorry." Then they'd lean in and whisper, "How are you doing?"

I called it being almost famous. Simply bringing up Bobby's death gave me an automatic out. My grief allowed me to be immune to others' needs. Sorrow was like a child's pacifier, allowing me to wallow in sadness, holding on to the security of my feelings at the time. The comfort of not growing, not moving on—I could get used to that.

But just as a child must eventually give up the pacifier, I'd have to allow God to work on my spirit to heal it. Like the tooth decay which must be dug out to have a healthy tooth, God's fingers needed room to work on my broken heart. I'd read in our Grief Share book about getting stuck in grief, unable to fully heal.

If I held on to my notoriety, I could keep my almost-famous status, but at what cost?

I've met mothers who can't—or won't—let go of their grief. Years pass, yet the child's room is still untouched, like a shrine. They cry over the gradual fading of their child's smell on the pillow. They refuse to part with even one thing which belonged to their son or daughter. Every birthday, anniversary, or holiday becomes sepia-toned as they wallow in the abyss of *what if?* and *why?*

The tendency can be to cling to grief as a way of setting oneself apart. As time passed, I lost my notoriety, my differentness. Other people forgot my loss. Their lives moved on as they faced their own difficulties and joys. I couldn't continue to bring up Bobby's death, although my craving for an opportunity to talk about it was still there.

Eventually, I found the challenge was to use my perceived differentness to grow. How difficult it was, when all around others were festive, and I wanted only to hide in a darkened room. December's sunny days warmed my body, but the coldness of death lingered in my spirit. Instead of green, red, and gold, I wished for a world of gray. Celebrating Christmas just wasn't right.

The vividness of Christmas decorations was like a shard of glass in my eye.

Mike insisted we pull ourselves out of the pit of despair and do something different on Christmas Day. We prepared a lavish brunch and invited my brother and his wife to drive up for the day from the Bay Area. My mom and a couple of friends joined us too.

My brother told the story of his miraculous healing after suffering a heart attack. He shared how he'd turned his life over to Jesus after the doctors told him he'd survived because he had the heart of a twenty-one-year-old.

In addition to heaving a sigh of relief when the day was over, I breathed a prayer of thanks to God for the blessing of the day. Everything from Thanksgiving to New Year's was different, but all of them were good. Sadness was kept at bay as we survived another first.

Jerry Sittser, in *A Grace Disguised,* talks about how we grow from loss. Loss reminds us, too, how meaningful life can be even through our suffering. Even though Bobby and Dad couldn't be with us for the holiday celebrations, I rejoiced over my brother's amazing testimony.

Shortly after the holidays, I dreamed about Bobby again. I was in a house with a pool. I stepped out to go swimming, but the day was already dark, and the pool lights weren't on. I called out for Mike to turn on the lights, but he didn't answer. I heard Bobby's voice, and followed the sound to where he was, lounging in a hot tub. He was totally bald, and his eyebrows were nonexistent. He told me, "The reason I came back is I have things I want to say."

"Good," I said. "I have things to say to you before you go away forever."

I must have been frustrated over what had been left unsaid.

The irony is when someone dies, your life is profoundly changed because of their death, and yet they're the very one you want to share the changes with. How many times I wanted to call Bobby to tell him how God was working through my loss. His death wasn't some random luck of the draw or some divine drawing of lots. The purpose wasn't yet obvious, but I knew God didn't mean it for my harm. I longed for Bobby's reassurance everything would be okay.

In Psalm 139, my favorite section of Scripture says this: "Your eyes saw my substance, being yet unformed. And in Your book they all were written, the days fashioned for me, when as yet there were none of them" (Psalm 139:16).

Bobby's days were numbered before he was born. God wasn't taken by surprise by his early death. Cancer didn't happen when God wasn't looking. Cancer didn't happen because of something I did or didn't do.

Bobby said this to me about six months before he passed. "I always knew I would die young. I just didn't think I would die *this* young."

Is this the same kid who threw a fit when it was his turn to do the dishes? The one who almost burned the house down by lighting fireworks in his room? The maturity of his statement was hard for me to imagine, coming from such a wild child.

What would I do if I knew my death was imminent?

Would I whine to God about my unfair lot in life? Or cry and cling to bitterness? No one knows how they might respond in any situation. My gratitude goes to Bobby for showing me how a man of God acts in the face of extreme adversity.

My loss has pressed out my faith. I had nowhere else to turn except to the giver of life. I felt weak and unable to cope for many months after Bobby entered into eternity. Everything seemed hard. My emotions rose quickly to the surface. I'd feel anger, frustration, and sorrow—all in the space of an hour. Still, I continually reminded myself every circumstance coming my way was part of a greater scene I couldn't and, in some ways still can't, see.

In C. S. Lewis's book, *The Great Divorce*, he talks about one blade of grass in a huge meadow as our lives and our world, compared to the entire creation of God. We think our one blade of grass is everything. To God, it's only a minuscule part, but we feel like our tiny portion is the whole.

I'm reminded of the time a friend and I sat in Starbucks having coffee. She asked how I was doing. I put my finger on the edge of the table, right in the middle between the two sides.

"This is my life, and his life," I told her. "The rest of the table represents eternity. I have the entire table to spend with Bobby once this little space of time is done."

I'd come a long way in eight months.

***

When he passed away, I didn't know how to survive the next thirty or so years before my time to go arrived. Assuming I'd live into my eighties, like my parents and grandparents, thirty years seemed a terribly long wait. I had to continually remind myself of the verse, "For I consider that the sufferings of this present time are not worthy to be compared with the glory that is to be revealed to us" (Romans 8:18 NASB).

Henry Nouwen in his book, *Can You Drink the Cup*, reminds us in the midst of sorrows is consolation, in the midst of the darkness is light, and in the midst of despair is hope.

God's grace brings hope to the sufferer. "Blessed are those who mourn, For they shall be comforted" (Matthew 5:4).

A time eventually came when Bobby's death wasn't in my mind's forefront. Eventually sunlight burned through the fog, bringing a glimpse of hope. Still, like a landmine in a field of flowers, grief still caught me unaware. Some days, the smallest thing made me weep. A song, a phrase, a memory—any of these could trigger a deluge of tears.

When a loved one dies, everything seems to remind us of them. Their presence permeates our homes, cars, even public places.

Remember when we ate there together?

We shopped for shoes at that store.

Do you remember the time ...?

Every memory clutches the heart, squeezing with a giant hand.

Those sharp stabs of remembrance are impossible to avoid. Over time the pain lessens, and the sharpness becomes a dull ache. If we allow God to help us work through the pain, we'll move into a place where memories bring joy, not sorrow. He promises us as much in his Word.

"Weeping may endure for a night, but joy comes in the morning" (Psalm 30:5).

CHAPTER 11

THE LIGHT AT THE END OF THE VALLEY

Through Facebook, I reconnected with a friend who attended the same church as I did in the late '80s and early '90s. The church grew rapidly from a small home meeting to several hundred people, all in the space of a few years. We believed we were riding a new wave of the Spirit of God. God was doing a new thing in our midst. The pulpit message of that day was God wants you to be healthy and wealthy. If you were, it was a sign of God's blessing. If you had health issues or had financial setbacks, the time had come to examine your heart for unconfessed sin. Perhaps you needed to tithe more, or you needed to break a generational curse of sickness and lack.

Everything changed when the pastor was diagnosed with lung cancer. Suddenly, the message was different. No longer were the infirm and financially struggling looked at with judgment. Mercy and grace flowed through the church body like a stream of water carving a path in a dry creek bed. When the pastor died a year later, we mourned together. Several of us from the church kept in contact through the years. Facebook made it much easier.

I read on Facebook my friend's daughter, Loni, had died. She was the same age as Bobby. She died five months after he did. Susanne, Loni's mother, struggled with the *why?* question for a long time. Their daughter's autopsy couldn't pinpoint a cause of death—no physical reason for this healthy thirty-year-old woman to die in her sleep. Loni had a vibrant ministry to the youth in her church. She was a gifted musician with a voice which drew people to the Spirit. How could this happen?

Susanne agonized over the circumstances surrounding Loni's passing. Her body wasn't discovered for over twenty-four hours. When friends realized they hadn't heard from her, which was unusual, they went to her apartment and found her. Susanne didn't know if Loni struggled before she died or if she was scared or if she was aware she was alone.

Everything Susanne knew about God was turned upside down. Only by his grace did she survive.

We mothers ask the question, "My child was a good person. Why did he die? Why did she die?" The question should be not *why,* but *why not*? Why do we think good people are immune to tragedy? God's word is filled with stories of regular people who faced terrible circumstances. King David and Job lost children to death. The apostle Paul was put in prison more than once. Stephen was stoned. Even today, our Christian brothers and sisters in Asia and Africa face starvation, death, and homelessness, and not always in the name of Christ.

Someone asked a few months ago about the main thing I took from the experience of losing Bobby. Without thinking, I blurted, "My world isn't safe. I'm not immune from catastrophe." I'd lost my innocence. I'd always thought if I lived my life as a good Christian, I'd walk through life, while not unscathed, certainly not vulnerable to disaster.

My ability to look at life through rose-colored glasses has been stripped from me. Instead, I search for danger lurking in the shadows, careful to avoid dark corners and sharp edges to avoid being hurt again. Every car ride has the potential to end in an accident. Any phone call could bring bad news. If Mike is late coming home, I picture him slumped over from a heart attack.

And yet, by God's grace, I continue to live as a victor, knowing he is there with me in every circumstance. Having the worst tragedy happen to me didn't immunize me from future calamity. I don't have to look very hard to find places where the holes opened up, threatening to swallow me.

But God.

I love those two words. God wouldn't let me stay in the valley of the shadow of death. His rod and staff prodded me to the end of the valley—toward the light. He requires constant forward motion for his people. If we stay in one place, we stagnate.

Shepherds, to keep their sheep healthy, move their flocks to higher ground when the summer sun scorches the grazing grass to brown. The shepherd herds them up narrow mountain trails, careful to nudge them away from the edges and precipices so they don't fall.

The way is steep. The sheep grow tired of climbing and rebel against the daily hike. The shepherd must use his rod and staff as a means of discipline to keep his flock in line for their own good. Eventually the sheep safely reach the high pastures, where green grass is abundant, the air is crisp, and the water sweet.

Just like the sheep in the Old Testament, I had to keep moving on to higher, more fertile ground, to feed and grow strong again.

Through my bereavement, I've found the truth of Psalm 23:3—God restores my soul. After spending much time with him alone, pouring out my grief like sour lemon juice, he has restored my soul as I enter the higher ground—knowing with God I can face any circumstance.

***

As February and March approached, trepidation grew over the first "anniversaries." My dad had died February 16th. I wondered how strong I'd need to be for my mom. Surely, she'd fall apart. They'd been married almost sixty-seven years when he passed. She'd taken care of everything until he went to live in the assisted living care home.

As it turns out, she handled the one-year anniversary better than I did. We cried together that day, but she was peaceful, knowing Dad was free from the pain he'd had on earth. However, March loomed in my path. Bobby's birthday, March 19th, and his death day, March 29th. My anxiety began to grow—like the cancer which had grown in Bobby's chest.

I'd decided to make a scrapbook of my favorite photos of him from birth to death, digging through our huge box of photos and memories, struggling to pick just the right ones. Tears blurred the images of him proudly holding up the first fish he caught, falling asleep still wearing a motorcycle helmet at four years old, and as a teenager, showing off his bloody hand from a mountain biking accident.

Have you ever taken on a project which started out being fun, but over time began to drag on and on? Somewhere in the middle, you got bogged down, either because it was harder than you expected, or other commitments made you want to just get it done.

That's how my Bobby scrapbook was. At first, my thought was how wonderful it would be to capture his life and all the highlights. I could look at it from time to time throughout the years, remembering fun times, and show it to my grandchildren to remind them of Uncle Bobby. It would be a tribute to him.

I had no idea how hard it would be. Some days, I was only able to stare at the photos and cry. The scrapbook sat unfinished on my worktable for weeks. I felt guilty because it wasn't getting done. I wouldn't even work on new pages for my grandkids' scrapbooks, because there was this huge, looming project staring at me. It was just a scrapbook. Why get so worked up over it? I'd made several scrapbooks, one or two for each of my grandchildren, one for our trip to Spain, one for Mexico, and one for miscellaneous family photos.

I usually take time to make each page of my scrapbooks fun and cute. This one had become a chore. One night, I decided just to slap those photos in and call it finished. Whew! Weight off the shoulders. Relief in my spirit.

The good thing is, I know Bobby would understand and say, "No worries, Mama."

As Bobby's birthday approached, I told my staff I'd be taking a sick day. I watched the memorial video shown at the reception after his service, the video that makes me cry to this day. I thumbed through the scrapbook, thought of all the things I never got to say, and wondered if I'd said "I love you" enough. I fretted about the next first—the first anniversary of his death.

The same night, in a vivid dream, Bobby and I walked alongside each other.

"I love you," I said, and when he said, "I love you too, Mama," I knew there wouldn't be any more regrets.

I've talked to many women who've experienced the death of a child. Each one told of the difficulty of the firsts. The first Christmas, the first birthday, the first day of school. The ones whose lost children had been a bit older spoke of watching their child's friends graduate from high school.

When I see mothers and sons together, a pang of jealousy rises up.

That should be me.

I wish I could be the one to stand proudly beside my darling boy.

Bobby used to grab my hand when we'd walk together. We'd be in a mall, or heading into a movie theater, and he'd unashamedly take my hand. His tenderness stirred my proud mom's heart. *Look,* I wanted to shout. *My adult son isn't embarrassed to hold my hand.*

These memories, these recollections which make me smile, are God's grace to me. During the first several months after his death, I wondered if I'd ever be able to bring something to mind without crushing sadness. Thanks be to God, whose unending grace helped me walk through the valley toward the light.

★★★

What is it about grief which either separates us from others or brings us closer together? There's no wishy-washy middle ground. For those of us who've lost someone close, grief still lurks around every corner, waiting to pounce. A song, a special time of day, a fleeting memory—these are the things which bring tears to the eyes and longing to the heart. When we meet others who've lost a child, the connection is immediate. We know without saying a word the depths of their sorrow. Others who haven't felt the pain may avoid us for fear of being sucked into our grief or fear of saying the wrong thing.

Before Bobby's death, I either mouthed the expected platitudes to bereaved friends—*I'm sorry for your loss. You'll see your loved one again*—or simply didn't acknowledge their loss at all. Unsure of what to say, I'd skip over any reference to the one who'd died, afraid to bring it up, afraid I'd cause more pain.

Now that I'm on the other side, I appreciate those who remember Bobby. I worked with a woman years ago when Bobby had cancer the first time, and after I moved on to another employer, our paths would occasionally cross. "How's your son?" was always her first question. She was the only one who ever asked. Now he's gone, she's not hesitant to bring up his name when we meet.

We must teach others—grief can't be avoided and won't be ignored. When we show others how we grieve, we show them how to live beyond the feeling. Grief, loss, suffering—all are part of our human existence, all part of God's omnipotent plan. It is possible to experience affliction, yet secure little or no blessing from it. I could have chosen to rail against God for letting my son die. I could have let myself be a victim of circumstances, instead of a recipient of God's grace.

There was nothing I could have done to change the outcome of Bobby's life. What I did or didn't do could make no difference in how long or how short the time he lived. What I chose to do was to rest in Christ and receive comfort from him in my suffering. I had to surrender myself and my own self-will. As soon as I said, "This isn't fair. Life shouldn't be this way," I knew I'd slipped back into being a victim.

I heard an evangelist years ago who told of meeting someone for the first time.

"How are you doing?" he asked the person.

The response was, "Okay, under the circumstances."

"What are you doing under there?" demanded the evangelist.

This has stuck with me for over twenty years. I don't want to be under my circumstances. It only makes me a victim instead of a victor.

Our American culture says we're strong individuals. We can take anything and get back up. The surge of patriotism after September 11, 2001, is a prime example of how we rise from the ashes, arms swinging toward the enemy. Sometimes, I think we in the church feel we should rise strong, be victorious, and put our best face forward, no matter what.

Then, we become plastic people with fake smiles and empty words.

It's so much easier to do what I call the drive-by greeting.

"Hey, Sue, how's it going?" I say, as I arrive at the church doors and wave in Sue's direction. "Fine" is the answer I expect to receive as I rush into the worship service. Any other response would slow me down, make me listen, and make me give something of myself. This is typical of our American churches.

That's why I'm grateful for my fellow Grief Sharers. We wept together and held each other up. We didn't have to put on a triumphant face. We were vulnerable and spoke about our uncertainties of going on without our loved one. We'd been sucker punched, but we helped each other up. We encouraged each other not to remain "under the circumstances." We got up, knees wobbling, steps tentative, leaning heavily on each other's arms.

Many people say death is the Christian's enemy. I don't agree. Jesus came to break the terror of death. When we know Jesus, death is simply exchanging this finite life for everlasting life. This is how we can comfort others, even during our loss.

Mothers, if you aren't sure if your child was a believer in Jesus at the time of his or her death, take comfort when I tell you only God knows the state of your child's heart at the moment they left this earth. I don't know if my dad heard me yell in his ear as he was dying. I don't know if he understood my final plea for him to turn to Jesus. God is the only one who knows.

I comfort myself with the knowledge the answer is ultimately in God's hands.

CHAPTER 12

THE YEAR AFTER

I have vivid dreams. They can be either a blessing or a curse, depending upon whether they're happy or sad. Sometimes the dream doesn't make any sense, and I wake up thinking, *what was that all about?*

I've dreamed a lot about Bobby. One in particular sticks in my mind. I was rubbing his tummy because that was where the cancer had spread. I knew he'd die soon, but at the same time I knew he'd already died. I told him, "This time I want to tell you all the things I didn't get to say before. I'll miss you every single day. Sometimes, I'll cry and sometimes, I won't, but I'll think of you every day."

He answered, "I'm going to miss you so much."

"No, you won't," I answered. "You'll be in heaven. There's no sadness there."

"I'll think about you all the time."

"You're leaving a huge hole in our family," I said.

He began to cry, and I woke up sobbing.

As time went on, I dreamed about him less and less. I miss those little reunions. I don't know if dreams are strictly from our subconscious, or if God sometimes sends them to either comfort us or help us work through our grief. I do know even when I woke up crying, I was grateful for being able to see Bobby again.

When I look at how God works in my life, I must admit his work can be inconvenient at times. Bobby's death was inconvenient for all concerned. Inconvenient for my husband to lose his job two months later. Inconvenient for me, having to cook for my mom every night after my dad died.

But when I look at my life's circumstances as God's grace to me, I have to stop making the distinction between good and bad (inconvenient!) circumstances. Grace is defined as "undeserved favor."

How can these crummy, inconvenient circumstances be an undeserved favor? More like undeserved punishment.

And right there is where I have to stop regarding myself as the center of the universe—when I have to use my eyes of faith. The judgment between good and bad is not situational or circumstantial. Convenient or inconvenient, God's working in my life just *is*. I can either accept it with grace (there's that word again), or chafe against it. My choice? His grace.

I attended a conference a couple of weeks after returning from Bobby's memorial service in Colorado. I sat with a guy I'd met once, a business acquaintance. We recognized each other as the only person we knew at the event. We sat together, two almost-strangers, desperate to make a connection so we wouldn't feel alone.

I asked the usual questions. *How's business, what's new, what brings you to the event?* As we waited for the presentation to begin, we stumbled onto the subject of family. He couldn't stop talking about his son. The young man was a senior in high school and apparently, a jazz musician prodigy.

His words weren't the part bothering me. As he raved and raved about his son's musical ability, all I could think was, *what if he asks me how many kids I have?* My breathing quickened, and my hands started to sweat. I wiped them on my slacks under the table. His words blended together into buzzing as I considered my answer.

Do I say I only have one grown daughter? Do I go into any kind of detail such as, I had two, but now I only have one?

Around and around in my brain the thoughts whirled, like a sock dancing with the agitator in a washing machine. Head pounding, heart racing, I finally excused myself and raced for the door of the convention center, intent upon reaching the safety of my car. I climbed behind the wheel and took several shaky breaths.

"Get a grip," I told myself, as the panic attack continued to claw at me. Then the reality hit me—this would be a situation I'd face forever. I needed to come up with an answer, but my brain refused to cooperate.

In the early days after Bobby's death, I welcomed the opportunity to say, "My son passed away," loving the immediate sympathy, the almost-famous syndrome. I could get out of doing things for other people, being involved in church, helping, just by using my golden ticket. Who can argue with "My son died"?

I've met some lovely women who are stuck in the almost-famous syndrome. They carry their grief around like a battered suitcase with a broken wheel, marking a path in the valley of the shadow of death.

I didn't want to stay stuck in the valley, but at that moment, in the sanctity of my car, I didn't know how to escape. The doors were locked, and the windows were closed, and the car was sinking into a murky bog.

***

I've met women whose faith made me cry. Their children died young—some due to tragic circumstances—and yet these mothers are filled with grace. My thoughts go back to the woman whose daughter Andrea died at twelve years old. What was originally thought to be a drowning accident in their backyard swimming pool turned out to be an undiagnosed heart infection. The autopsy results took six months—a lifetime, when a death seems unexplainable.

What began as her unspeakable tragedy turned into a vibrant ministry to other parents whose children died. She and her husband provide care boxes filled with paper plates, napkins, plastic ware, and other peripheral things often not considered among the flood of food and visitors when someone dies. Lynn's provision has opened numerous doors for her to offer hope to a hurting family. She shares the love of Jesus, if they are receptive, or simply gives them a shoulder to cry on and a hug. Her experience gives her instant connection.

Many times, during the months following Bobby's passing, a cloud seemed to follow my every move, weighted with the rain of tears I'd cry if only I could work up enough energy. My grief needed to be purged, but even that was too much effort. Instead, I'd open the wine and numb my senses. Crying took too much energy—energy I needed to drag myself through the days of emptiness.

How long would I feel this way? How long until anger and grief faded, like the childish drawings hung on the wall as a monument to his life? How long until I could smile at a memory without melancholy tagging along behind? Would grief and joy forever be joined, like Siamese twins, sharing one heart?

Before Ali cut off communication with us, she sent a tiny urn containing some of Bobby's ashes. This is what her note said:

> I'm sending you a little package of love! In the box is a keepsake for you of Robert's ashes. When he told me where he wanted his ashes spread, I reminded him how

crazy of a hike it was to get to that lake and that everyone wouldn't be able to make it. He said, "That's okay, give them a little cup of my ashes. Tell them it's a piece of my left leg, some toes, and a piece of my heart."

That's my boy.

I dreamed of him more often. He was always dying. In one dream, Bobby told me, "I'd really like to stay and hang around the family a little longer."

Yes, I'd like that too. There's a theme running through the dreams.

I'm glad you came back for a little while, so I could tell you all the things I didn't say before.

★★★

A mother's intuition is a mystery. Is it because we carry the child in our own body for nine months, intimately joined in the closest way possible? We know every nuance of our children's faces. We know when they're on the verge of a meltdown. We know when they've had a bad day at school. We recognize every change of expression. We're trained observers and amateur psychologists. We predict which situation will become a battle of wills. We know how to make our child smile. The only thing we can't predict?

When our child will die.

My world was rocked by my son's death. Even though he didn't live under our roof, in our home, or even in our state, his part in our family web was empty. Heather lost her best friend, the one person who connected to her childhood. There wouldn't be any family gatherings where they could laugh over childish pranks and how they'd pulled one over on Mom and Dad.

Part of what I lost was my pride in my son. He'd grown into a man others adored. He served in his church. He was faithful to his wife. He started his own business and bought his first house. I was proud of what he'd become. I bragged about him and his sister, how they did things right by not having sex with their spouses before marriage. How they'd saved to buy a home.

I still have my daughter to brag on, but part of my pride and joy died with Bobby. When people now ask me how many children I have, many times I answer, "Just one. A daughter." If I don't know them well, explaining about my loss is too difficult—a conversation stopper for sure. Sometimes, I just don't want the sympathy. Other times, I do.

When I say I have only one child, I wonder if people look at me funny. Not that I think any less of friends who have one child. But it's different when the idea is turned in my direction. Perhaps others think there's something physically wrong with me, or I'm selfish for having just one child. Or whatever. I cringe inwardly, almost as if admitting to some secret fault.

I know it sounds crazy. But it's there.

Such a stark contrast to when he first passed away. I wanted the world to know how much I hurt. I felt like climbing up on my roof and shouting, "Hey! Listen up, world. My son died. Feel sorry for me. Acknowledge my loss." I'd join in every conversation, waiting for the opportunity to jump in and vomit my pain onto others.

I've learned this is normal, but normality doesn't take away the ugliness. Heaving my grief onto friends, acquaintances, and anyone else who would listen was a way for me to get others to shoulder my pain—a way to keep Bobby alive a little longer.

As I've mentioned, God requires forward movement. We call this growth. He expects us to continue to become conformed to the image of his son, Jesus.

A story about a famous sculptor says visitors watched in fascination as the artist took a solid piece of marble and began to form a sculpture of a horse. One of the spectators asked, "How do you do it? How can you take this block of unformed rock and create a beautiful horse?"

The sculptor answered, "It's simple. I just chip away anything that doesn't look like a horse."

Sounds simple, doesn't it? When I think of my Christian growth as a sculpture, I picture times when God has had to use a jackhammer to sledge off large pieces of me which don't resemble the end product, which is Jesus. Other times, he manages the fine work with exact tools and a small, ball peen hammer.

I found God's grace in the exacting work he did through Bobby's death and the sorrow shadowing me for the following year. Many times, I felt God's fingers pressing on a sensitive spot he wanted to change, reconfigure, and reform.

When we announced to our church fellowship of thirteen years we were leaving, our sorrow and relief blended together—sorrow to leave our spiritual family and friends but relief at not having to explain yet again how we still grieved over Bobby. I still wrestle with bitterness over the way we were treated. I felt my loss was minimized or equaled with others who'd experienced what seemed to me to be lesser losses. Some had lost positions of leadership. Some lost their freedom by having a baby. Another had a husband who had cancer but was returning to health. My loss was just one of many experiences within our little group.

But I didn't think so.

We decided to attend the church which had sponsored our Grief Share group. At first, we only knew the few who were part of Grief Share. But as we've served there, we now have a large circle of support. Our small group prays continually for us as life events set off spasms of sorrow.

Sometimes, a parent can predict how a situation will trigger their emotions. An invitation to a baby shower or a coworker's announcement of an unexpected pregnancy—either of these could ambush the heart of a woman whose baby died before birth. For the mother whose child died at twelve, the pain comes in watching her child's friends go from middle school to high school to college, knowing she won't experience any of those joys.

I never know when grief will ambush me. Sometimes, it's hearing a song on the radio Bobby and I both liked. Sorrow will hit me like a wave, knocking me into the sand, making me gasp for air. Other times, I'll think he'd really like the fact I'm fulfilling my dream of writing and publishing books. Then sorrow laps at my feet, a gentler wave reminding me he'll never see his mom's name on a book cover.

The year after a child's death is the worst, when you learn to live with what's called your "new normal." Mike and I talk about it like losing a finger. You eventually get used to having one less digit, but you'll always miss the part of you which made you whole. You can work around and compensate, seeming to cope on the outside. But sometimes you forget the finger's gone and try to do something requiring all ten fingers. Then reality bites again, grief takes over, and an adjustment needs to be made.

I'd like to say God's grace carried me every step of the way during that first year. Perhaps he did without my realizing it. Many weeks I hid behind sleep, alcohol, food—whatever gave me a smidge of comfort. I withdrew from friends, wouldn't attend required work functions, and barely kept myself together.

Other times, I put on a brave face and did what had to be done, operating on autopilot until I got home and crawled into my pajamas, then into bed.

I discovered who my true friends were. They were the ones who didn't abandon me when I withdrew. They gently pulled me out of the black cloud and brought in a ray of sunshine. They sent cards, even though Bobby had passed months before. When I expressed my sorrow and despair on my blog, their encouraging comments urged me to look up.

Devastating loss can separate us or bring us closer to others—like the sword of the Spirit, dividing even between bone and marrow. Some of the people we thought we could always rely on have faded away, as if our loss is somehow contagious. Others who've been on the fringes of our lives suddenly come to the forefront with open arms and hands full of grace. God's grace, in human form. What could be greater?

CHAPTER 13

GRANDMOTHERS AND SISTERS

Grandparents are an important part of a child's inheritance. Grandmothers, especially, hold a place in children's memories. We called my grandma Nini. She was no more than five foot one and weighed barely a hundred pounds, but she was a force to be reckoned with in our family.

We'd always lived near my mom's parents growing up. When I was born—the third child of Nini's only child, my mother—Nini took me as her own. She sewed all my clothes, taught me to sew when I was in high school, and spoiled her only girl grandchild rotten.

When Mike and I had our first child, Nini snatched her away too. Heather became her little great-grandchild doll. She made clothes for her, painted her toenails, and spoiled *her* rotten. Then Bobby came along, and my mom finally got her own grandchild to pamper and spoil. If Heather spent the night at Nini's, then Bobby had to spend the night at *my* mother's—his grandma's—house. Mike and I didn't complain. Free babysitting is priceless.

Bobby and Grandma became coconspirators, doing things Mom and Dad might not have approved of. Only later would we find out and wonder how they'd gotten away with it. Thus began the legends around the table at holiday dinner parties.

My mom couldn't contain her grief the first time Bobby was diagnosed with cancer. After our visit with the doctor, Mike immediately went to her house to tell her. The back of our house was across the alley from the back of my parents' house. Mike took the short walk, dreading having to tell my parents the diagnosis.

Mom doubled over in pain, crying over the unfairness of life. She became hysterical, unable to accept comfort because of the devastating news of Bobby's illness.

I wasn't there when Mike delivered the news of Bobby's cancer the second time. I was in the hospital waiting room, sobbing into the phone as I relayed the doctor's diagnosis. It was up to Mike to deliver the blow. Telling Mom this time was especially hard since my dad had passed away only three weeks earlier.

★★★

My mom misses Bobby's regular phone calls. He used to call her just to talk, bringing her up to date on his life. I never had to prompt him to call his grandma. He just did. She says sometimes her phone rings now and her heart jumps, thinking it might be him. Then she remembers.

The loss of a grandchild hits grandmothers especially hard. My mom still questions why Bobby had to die at thirty, while she continues to linger into her late eighties. She's lived a fulfilling life, yet Bobby's life had barely begun when it ended.

She's ready to go, to be with Jesus.

Only by God's grace can she accept his divine plan and trust he is working behind the scenes for his greater purpose. She's grateful Bobby knew his place in God's kingdom. She looks forward to seeing him again soon.

I spoke with a young grandmother who lost her four-year-old granddaughter to a brain tumor. The grandmother struggled with her own grief and was at a loss on how to comfort her son and his family. She told me it was difficult to watch her son suffer over the loss of his child after her long illness. The woman took comfort from Psalm 68:19–20, "Praise be to the Lord, to God our Savior, who daily bears our burdens. Our God is a God who saves; from the Sovereign LORD comes escape from death" (NIV).

"I'm an only child." Our daughter, Heather, feels the loss of her brother when she looks at her own children. She's saddened when she thinks about her kids not having a blood-related uncle to teach them some of the crazy games she and Bobby played as children.

"Remember when we ...?"

"Guess who I ran into the other day?"

"Did Mom and Dad ever find out about ...?"

No one else will remember the terror when they were playing in the trunk of a car and got stuck. No one else will share the relief when they got out.

Not only is part of Heather's shared history gone, but future memories will never be created.

During the year before Bobby died, God was already preparing Heather for the loss of her brother, though she was unaware of his work.

That year was one of transition for Heather and her husband—they'd sold their house and had to live in a basement apartment until remodeling on their new home was complete. Heather was pregnant with their third child, and she and her husband believed they were called to the mission field.

So much change gave Heather the opportunity to draw closer to God. She devoured books like *Crazy Love* and

Chasing Daylight. Living for God's eternal kingdom became her source of comfort and support. When the news of Bobby's imminent death became a reality, she already felt the strength of God's presence.

God's grace through Bobby's passing has given Heather the opportunity to share with a woman in her church whose sister died this year after a year-long battle with cancer. They're fellow members of the club of common loss.

God is at work in Heather, even through her sorrow.

CHAPTER 14

THREE YEARS AND COUNTING

"You're going to do what?"

My mom sat back in her chair, her face a mask of disbelief.

"I'm getting a tattoo. In memory of Bobby."

She shook her head, unable to comprehend why a woman in her fifties would permanently mark her body.

The three-year anniversary of Bobby's death was approaching. Mike and I talked about what we should do to commemorate the day. Then Bobby's best friend Mark called me.

"You've been threatening to get a tattoo for three years. I made an appointment for you. We're going together on his birthday."

I sat in the chair at the tattoo parlor, apprehensive yet determined. The artist showed me what the design would look like—the readout of a digital clock, 11:11, permanently engraved on the inside of my left wrist. Whenever I looked at my watch, I'd always think about Bobby time. Mark's tattoo was a grandfather clock with the hands in the 11:11 position. How amazing to know after three years, Bobby still had an impact on others' lives.

Bobby and Mark were like David and Jonathan in the Bible—not related by blood, but closer than brothers. The Bible says in Proverbs, "There is a friend that sticks closer than a brother." I don't know much about the brother-to-brother relationship. My brothers are much older than I am, and we've never had the kind of bond you think of when you hear the word *brother*.

But I do know about brother and sister relationships, at least the one my children shared. Heather and Bobby had a close relationship. Bobby said many times Heather was his best friend. As children they were often in cahoots with each other, keeping their antics from Mom and Dad.

But a friendship closer than a brother defies the DNA bond. Best friends don't have the sibling rivalry thing. They don't have a history of competing for their parents' attention. They can share personal struggles, knowing they won't be leaked to other family members. A friend offers an escape from the occasional dysfunction of familial relationships.

So, what happens when a friendship is torn apart through separation or an argument?

Or death?

There's a phrase people use when someone looks sad—*You look like you've lost your best friend.*

How true that statement is. It's like losing a limb, like losing a brother.

Brothers are there because they're born into our family. Their presence is out of our control. Friends are made incrementally, through the passage of time. When a friend is lost, they aren't easily replaced, as their unique relationship can never be replaced. Each person must learn to go on, seek new friends and new relationships, keeping the love in our hearts alive even as we grieve for the one who was lost.

Dan was the leader of our Grief Share group. He's the one who encouraged us to leave our small church fellowship and attend the church where he's the pastor of congregational care. His love and comfort were indicative of what we found when we joined his church. No longer were we criticized for talking about Bobby's death. Rather, we were encouraged to share our grief and receive comfort in return.

Then Stephanie, Dan's daughter, died suddenly at the age of twenty-three. The tables have turned, and now we're the ones doing the comforting. Reliving the grief and sorrow of Bobby's death is painful, as we cry together over our losses. Melancholy creeps in like a dark fog, obscuring the joy I've gradually discovered over these years. The flesh in me doesn't want to go back to those dark feelings. But at the same time, I look at where God has taken me from, and I'm grateful to be in this place of comfort.

The puzzle pieces once scattered and strewn across the table now form a discernible pattern. God's grace moved everything around so Dan and his wife could reach out and receive from me that which I received from others.

Dan's wife is now initiated into the secret club. She hates it as much as I do, but we have each other to love, comfort, and support.

After thirteen years, I don't stumble as much when asked how many children I have. My answers vary depending upon the situation. Sometimes, I'll say I have one daughter. Other times, my answer is "two children," and I immediately mention my three grandchildren, which usually keeps people from asking more questions. On rare occasions, I'll bring up Bobby's death. The responses are always the same—quick sympathy, then a change of subject.

Last year, I attended a writer's conference in Oregon and was placed with a roommate I'd never met. She was an older woman in her late seventies. She was writing a memoir of her husband's life. He'd died a few years earlier. I asked how he'd died, and her response was immediate.

"He died with grace."

No mention of a medical condition, tragic accident, or anything else. She was proud he died with dignity, never complaining about life's unfairness. I like that. When I mention Bobby's death, some ask how he died, and my answer never varies. I tell about the cancer which robbed him of his life.

In the days after he died, when people asked, I'd get angry and wonder why they didn't ask me how he lived rather than how he died. Because of that memory, when I talk to other mothers about their children, I say, "Tell me about him or her. What kind of person were they?"

Funny how those things don't bother me anymore. Although the dull ache of loss never leaves me, it only intensifies into sharp pain when something vividly reminds me he's gone.

Once in a while, the sky is the exact color of his eyes, the bluest of blue. Sometimes I'll see a young man, usually wearing a baseball cap, and I'll think, *that's Bobby!* I want to run to him and get a glimpse to see if it really is him. Then reality slaps like a wet towel across my face, and I remember he's gone.

Gone from sight, but not from my mind.

Gone from this world, but not from my heart.

Does any mother ever forget the child who's gone? I've talked with women who've had miscarriages, and they tell me whether the baby was a boy or girl, even though it was too early for an ultrasound. Something in their spirit knows. They may not talk about their miscarriage when someone asks how many children they have, but they hold that other tiny child in their heart, anxiously waiting for their reunion in Heaven.

Even women who have had abortions as teenagers or young adults talk about their baby being a boy or a girl, although this doesn't usually happen until much healing has taken place, and most commonly after a later-in-life salvation experience.

★★★

As mothers, we know our children. We're amateur child psychologists. We're mind readers.

We can predict the future.

"If you frown like that, your face will freeze that way."

"If you eat all your Halloween candy, your teeth will rot out of your head."

"Don't run into the street. You'll get hit by a car."

"You may hate your sister now, but one day you'll be best friends."

We're determined not to be our own mothers, yet we hear the same words come out of our mouths.

"Fasten your seatbelt. Drive carefully. Make good choices."

"Are you wearing that? *Really?*"

Motherhood exhausts us, tries every last bit of our patience, turns our hair gray, wrinkles our skin, and makes us wear completely uncool clothes. Some days, we'd like to trade our youngster in for a different model. We fantasize our baby was switched at birth with a good child.

Yet when a child dies, we feel robbed. Even if we didn't particularly like our offspring at the moment he or she was taken, our love is constant. We mourn the loss. We're filled with regrets at what should have or could have or might have been.

I wish I could have seen Bobby mature even more. I looked forward to seeing him and Ali change their minds about having children. Because of Bobby's massive radiation at seventeen and his obvious health issues, they'd decided not to try to have kids. Before he was sick, they briefly mentioned adopting a child from Africa. I held that conversation in my heart, hoping I'd have more grandchildren through the Daly side. He would have made a great dad. He was just a big kid around his nieces and nephews, who adored him. Like his own dad, kids flocked to Bobby because he was fun, always making up silly games to entertain.

After thirteen years, I still ask God why a good man like Bobby had to die. I've tried to convince myself many people were touched more by his death than his life. And I've suffered the guilt of feeling as though I've capitalized on his death by writing this book.

My *why?* question will not be answered this side of Heaven.

Sometimes, I wonder what I'd give to spend one more day with him. Would I relinquish ten years of my life for one day? Twenty years? Would I sacrifice my own life to save his?

I have no answers. All I know is God's grace is more real to me today than ever before.

Would I give up knowing God in a more personal and powerful way, if giving it up meant Bobby wouldn't have died?

No.

I wouldn't sacrifice my relationship with God for the benefit of having Bobby live. So difficult for me to write those words, yet deep in my spirit I know they're true. Do I wish it had happened differently? Absolutely.

Could there have been a better way?

In God's plan, the answer is no.

Everyone suffers loss. Our response to the loss either draws us closer to God or keeps us away. We naturally want to avoid loss because loss keeps us from being happy. If our goal is happiness, we not only stunt our own spiritual growth, but we fail to enter the suffering of others. God is more interested in our holiness than in our happiness. If we truly believe "In all things God works for the good of those who love him and are called according to his purpose," then we have to believe everything is either given to us by God, or allowed to pass through God's grace before it reaches us.

Everything given is ours to serve for our spiritual growth. I own all things which happen to me because they're for my good—contrary to the world's view.

★★★

Our American culture values personal happiness over personal growth. I think about the adults I know who are addicted to video games. They escape into a fantasy world, unable and unwilling to connect with their families. A spouse may be hurting and the children out of control, but the person refuses to let anything affect his pursuit of personal gratification.

I'm grateful to have a husband who has walked with me through the valley of the shadow of death. His path has been different and his grief more intense at times, but he knows the depth of loss. After Bobby died, things which used to matter to me in our relationship became irrelevant. Like every couple, we'd bicker over little things like who said what to whom, or *no, I told you that yesterday and you forgot* or *you never put your dishes in the dishwasher* or *why can't you ...?* The list goes on and on.

The bicker list fell away under the enormity of our shared loss. Being right ceased to matter to me. What difference did it make if he forgot to do something he said he'd do?

I saw Mike with new eyes. I saw a fellow sufferer. He mourned the loss of his golf partner. His dream of taking a cross-country bike trip with Bobby was no more. He missed Bobby's teasing reminders of his constant dieting, when he'd see Mike eating something sweet and ask, "Is this a cheat day, Dad?"

Our shared loss brought us closer together. I grieve on hearing about parents who get divorced after the death of a child. Their sorrow puts them on diverse paths. One—or both—refuses to acknowledge the other's pain and their own. The attempt to avoid pain drives them further and further apart. Their marriage becomes as fragile as an empty eggshell, easily crushed under bitterness and anger.

God's grace allowed me to see my husband in a new light. No longer was he annoying—instead, he was someone to cry with. Someone to enter my suffering as I entered into his. My personal happiness, which died along with Bobby, became of no importance. My need to be right and to be in control took a back seat to the grace given to me by God for my husband.

We pulled back from social events because of our shared grief. A few good friends continued to reach out but understood when we explained we just weren't very good company. Others made a few attempts, then moved on, leaving us behind. Many people who were our friends before Bobby died are now only distant memories. Sad to think our relationships weren't strong enough to endure our pain. Now we're gathering a smaller circle around us, bound by thick cords of shared grief. We're making new friends, finding them in unexpected places.

Grief Share talks about a "new normal." Nothing will ever be the same. Not only has my life changed outwardly by losing a child, but I've changed inwardly. While parts of the new normal feel like trying to force a square peg into a round hole, the inward changes are so profoundly positive I can hardly believe something so good could come out of such a devastating loss.

I used to be guilty of the drive-by prayer. Someone at church would ask me to pray for them during the week for a job interview, a difficult family situation, or a health issue. I'd agree, then maybe once or twice during the week, the person and their request would come to mind. I'd quickly send up a "Bless them, Lord" prayer so I could check the box. Yup, I prayed for them.

These days, I can't pray the drive-bys anymore. This cutting of my soul by God's scalpel has driven me deeper into prayer and meditation than ever before. My prayer, instead of "Bless them, Lord," is for the person to find Christ in whatever situation they find themselves. If the situation is a job interview, they might pray to be content whatever the outcome, resting in God's sovereign will and submitting to his omnipotence. If a health issue is the problem, they'd cling to Jesus and see him work in their situation, regardless of healing. I pray for them the same way I pray for myself, that God would use Bobby's death—and my reaction, response, and growth—for his glory. I pray others might see his grace through me as I've walked through the valley of the shadow of death and emerged battle-weary, yet victorious because he was beside me, before me, and behind me, leading and comforting along the way.

Grief will drop you to your knees. You'll collapse like a folding chair under the weight of your loss. While you're down on your knees, you'll either be crushed by sorrow, unable to stand up again, or you can spend time being washed in his grace. He will gently lift you and carry you through the season of sorrow until you can stand on your own.

The journey from grief to grace isn't easy. The valley of the shadow of death is a scary place to walk through. Just as in the old story of "Footsteps in the Sand," let God carry you through to the other side.

CHAPTER 15

Thirteen Years Later

Earlier, I mentioned the adage *time heals all wounds.* When you lose a child, you ask the question, "Does it? Does this wound heal?"

The answer is yes and no.

A few years ago, I broke the ring finger on my left hand. I was swinging into a beautiful blue lagoon from a thick rope in the island country of Vanuatu. My hand slipped, and I ended up with a spiral fracture requiring surgery and pins to repair the damage.

Six years later, the pain is gone, but the scar remains as a reminder of my clumsiness. When the weather changes, the metal pins ache. Time has healed the wound, but the ache resurfaces. The grief of losing a son or daughter is the same.

Sometimes, I see something unusual, and I think, "Bobby would love this." Then I remember he's no longer a part of my present or my future. Other mothers ask if the pain ever goes away, and my answer is the pain will grow less and be more bearable, but there will always be an empty spot in the family portrait.

I still stumble to answer the question, 'How many children do you have?' My answer depends on the audience. I've found, in sharing my story, women who have experienced the same loss are quick to share theirs. There's an instant bond, a sisterhood of mutual heartbreak.

I still dream about him. Sometimes he's still a little boy, usually around eight to ten years old. In other dreams, he's an adult. I love these little visits. I spoke with a mother yesterday who told me about one of her twin boys who died just hours after he was born. She dreams about the little boy she lost. We wondered together if the dreams we have are God's way of comforting us. The veil between this life and the next is gossamer thin. Could it be possible our children are part of the great cloud of witnesses mentioned in Hebrews 11?

I'd like to think so.

I won't know for sure until I step into eternity.

As I write these words, the United States is reeling from yet another elementary school shooting. My heart aches for those parents who sent their children to school as on any other day, expecting them to return home. Too many children die from senseless tragedies like this. It is unnatural for parents to have to bury their child because of tragic situations, whether the occurrence is a school shooting, an accidental fentanyl overdose, murder, or suicide.

I talk to what seems an increasing number of women who have experienced the loss of a child. A few months ago, a chance encounter with a couple turned into an opportunity to comfort them. The husband and wife looked like a typical Silicon Valley couple—nice clothes, perfect hair, sparkly jewelry. As the conversation turned from 'nice to meet you' to 'what's your story,' I learned their fifteen-year-old son had committed suicide a few months earlier. Mike and I cried with them as they shared their devastation.

God took our chance meeting and moved it to a deeper place. We parted ways knowing sharing our loss and slow healing meant they also would someday find healing.

My prayer, as you read this book and hear my story—and Bobby's—is you too might learn how God's grace can turn your worst loss into something beautiful. I never would have thought I'd believe the words from Romans 8:28— "And we know that all things work together for good to those who love God, to those who are the called according to His purpose."

May you find the good in all things your heavenly Father has for you.

ABOUT THE AUTHOR

What do you call a sixty-something woman who sells everything to travel full time in a motor home—crazy? Quirky? She proudly carries both descriptions. Jane writes from a deep sense of God's redemptive power, having witnessed it in her own life. When she isn't hunched over her computer, she can be found discovering unique places and amazing people in her journey to visit all lower forty-eight states.

Follow Jane's journey by signing up for her newsletter:

http://www.janesdaly.com

https://www.facebook.com/janedalyspeakerandauthor

https://www.instagram.com/thejanesdaly/

JANE'S OTHER ELK LAKE BOOKS

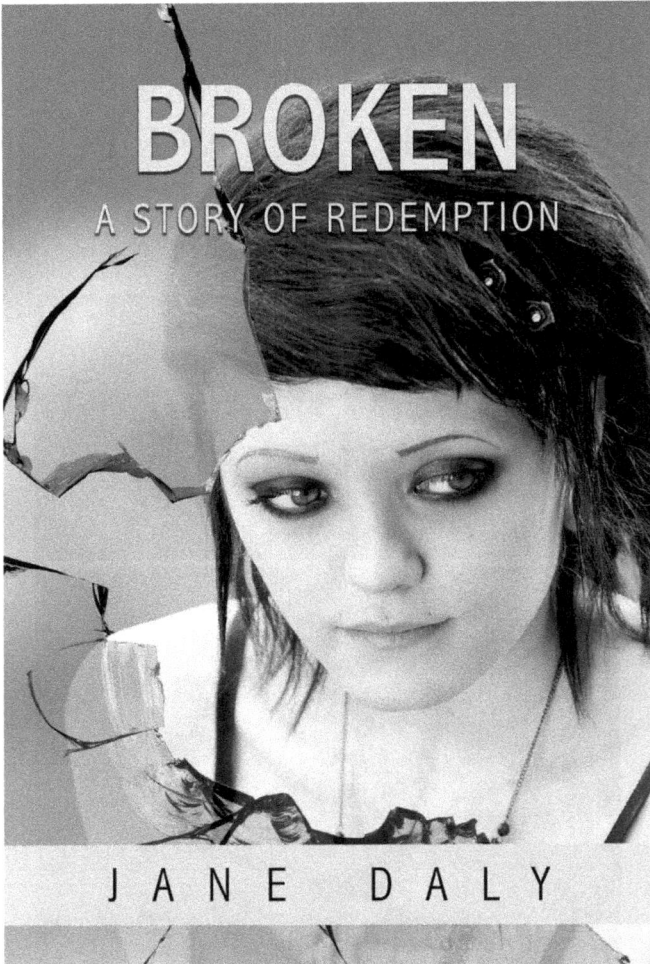

BROKEN

A STORY OF REDEMPTION

JANE DALY

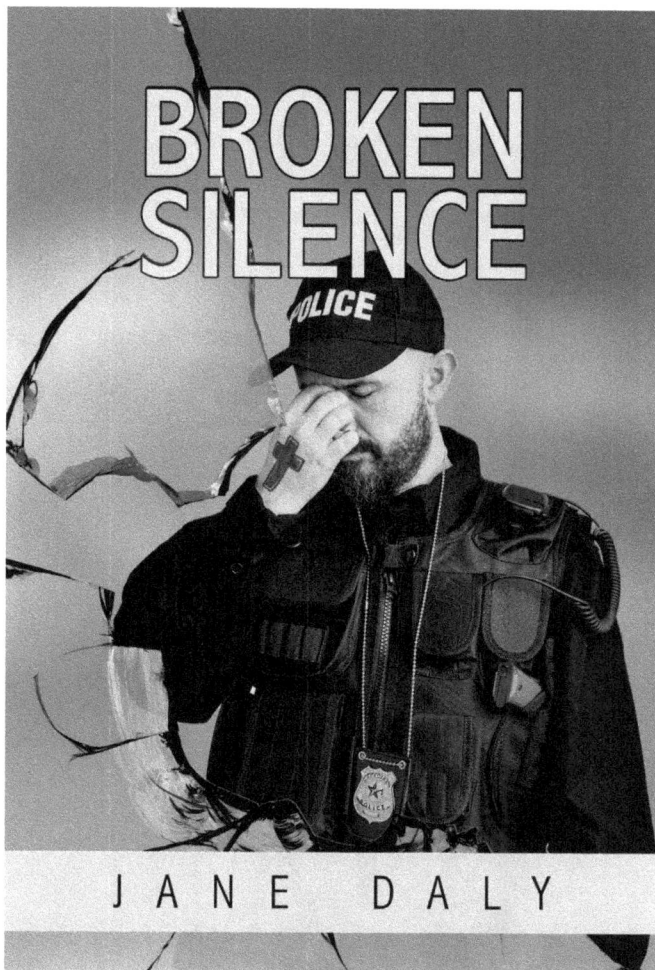

BROKEN
SILENCE

POLICE

J A N E   D A L Y

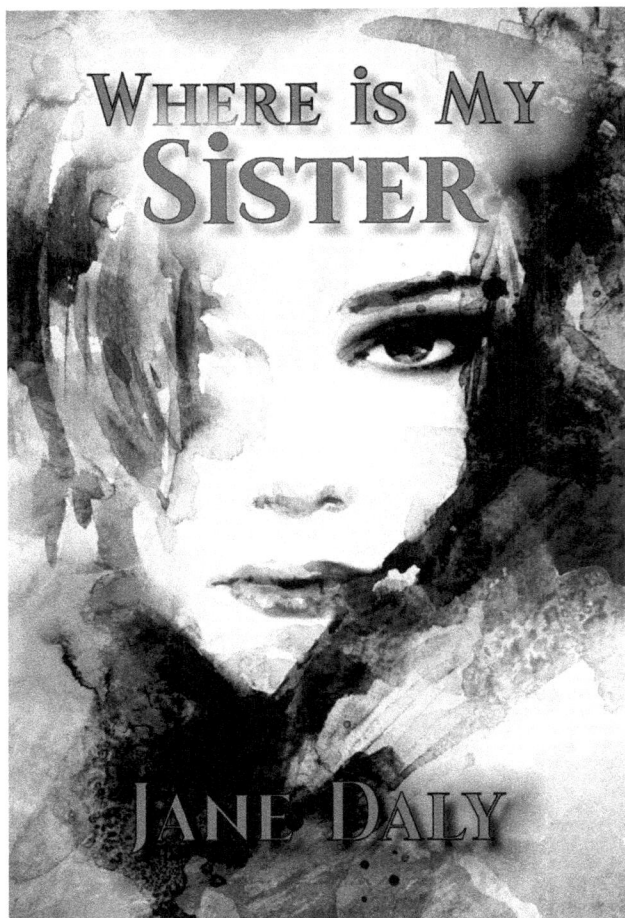

www.ingramcontent.com/pod-product-compliance
Lightning Source LLC
Chambersburg PA
CBHW071758090426
42737CB00012B/1872